An
Anthology
of Lunar Poetry

MOONSTRUCK

Selected and with an Introduction by
ROBERT PHILLIPS

The Vanguard Press, Inc.
New York

Library of Congress Catalogue Card Number: 73-83042
ISBN 0-8149-0734-2

Designer: Ernst Reichl
Manufactured in the United States
of America

FOR MARYA ZATURENSKA
AND HORACE GREGORY

CONTENTS

III   Lunar Masks

IV   The Bright Side

V The Dark Side

VI After Apollo

ACKNOWLEDGMENTS

I

For suggesting, even campaigning for, certain poems included here I am grateful to that apostle of poetry, Mr. Charles H. Willard, of Guilford, Connecticut. Thanks is also due the dedicatees, Mr. and Mrs. Horace Gregory, of Palisades, New York. I am indebted for counsel to Miss Emma Cohn, the New York Public Library, and to Mr. Thomas Woll, my editor, The Vanguard Press.

Once again Judith Bloomingdale, my wife and the Muse behind the laurel, has helped beyond possibilities of acknowledgment.

II

I have made every effort to trace the ownership of all copyright material and to secure permission from the holders of the copyright. In the event of any question arising from the use of a selection, the publisher and I, while expressing regret for any inadvertent error, will be happy to make the necessary correction in future printings or editions.

I gratefully acknowledge permission to reprint the following poems with thanks to the following individuals and publishers:

To Jack Anderson
   "Aesthetics of the Moon" by Jack Anderson. From *Inside Outer Space*, Robert Vas Dias, ed. Copyright © 1970 by Robert Vas Dias. Reprinted by permission of the poet.
To Atheneum Publishers, Inc.
   "Last Quarter" by John Hollander. From *Types of Shape* by John Hollander. Copyright © 1967 by John Hollander. Reprinted by permission of Atheneum Publishers. Appeared originally in *Partisan Review*.
   "The Creation of the Moon" translation by W. S. Merwin. From *Selected Translations 1948–1968* by W. S. Merwin. Copyright © 1958, 1968 by W. S. Merwin. Reprinted by permission of Atheneum Publishers.

Clouds now and then
 giving men relief
  from moon-viewing.

—*Matsuo Masho*
(Tr. Bownas & Thwaite)

. . . the history of poetry in
all ages is the attempt to
find new images for the moon.
 —*J. Isaacs,*
  THE BACKGROUND OF
  MODERN POETRY

INTRODUCTION

Before there was man there was the moon.

Before the discovery of fire the moon was man's only defense against the mysteries and dangers of the night. Man came to depend upon the moon for telling the time of day and the time of year, for the time of planting and the time of picking of crops. It is no wonder man elevated the moon to the status of god or goddess. It is no wonder Stone Age man performed religious rites in her honor.

Later, the moon became man's Muse as well. No poem in ancient Greece was deemed worthy that did not begin with a direct invocation to the moon-goddess.

It is the moon's role as Muse that makes this anthology possible and, I maintain, necessary. There have been perhaps no more frequent allusions in poetry than those to the moon. Voyages to the moon have been written about at least since Lucian's *Vera Historia* (circa A.D. 160). Nearly every poet worthy of the title (not to mention the June/Moon rhymers) seems to have struck a moon ode, himself moonstruck.

This anthology makes visible shifts in man's perspective on the moon through the centuries. She has been menacing and friendly, hideous and beautiful, wanton and chaste, male and female. To all, however, the moon remained mysterious. She was, in the words of the 17th-century poet Henry Vaughan, "that beauteous Queen, which no age tames."

Yet on July 20, 1969, at 4:17:40 P.M. EDT, man indeed "tamed" her—while all the world watched her surrender over television. And that which once had been supremely romantic has never since seemed the same. The goddess had been violated by mere man.

Certainly the Apollo landings have changed the course of poetry, as this anthology's final section verifies. The moon landings made earth itself a heavenly body. Myth-critic Joseph Campbell goes so far as to say "all poetry now is archaic that fails to match the wonder of this view." The astronauts themselves have spoken of observing the "earthrise"—a new image indicative of our shifting metaphorical perspective.

This book gathers poems to and about the moon from pre-Stonehenge to post–Sea of Tranquility. To my knowledge no other comprehensive lunar anthology in English has appeared. (*Adam: International Review* devoted a portion of an issue to moon poetry in 1969, the year of the first moon landing; and Robert Vas Dias's 1970 paperback anthology, *Inside Outer Space*, contains a number of lunar poems within its specialized format of "New Poems for the Space Age.")

I have tried to select for the poem, not the poet. For this reason some very great poets, as well as some very famous ones, are not represented. These wrote about the moon not particularly well. For instance, Carl Sandburg's *Collected Poems* displays a constellation of moons; yet none is so good as Sandburg on more earthly subjects. On the other hand, some unknown poets are found here. The Muse seems to have served them well.

Moreover, I have not printed poems that merely mention the moon, however arresting such mention may be. I have attempted to choose works that have not already appeared too frequently in anthologies. Reading for this anthology has refreshed my sense of certain poets too often omitted from recent collections—Longfellow, Lindsay, and Teasdale, for instance. It is my hope readers of this book will "rediscover" them as well.

Sequence is not chronological: such order prevents effective and fresh juxtaposition of different authors and views. Given the wealth of moon poetry, I have tried to represent each poet by no more than one poem apiece, that being the one I consider his best on the subject (a translation by a poet of another's poem is absolved from this rule). A few moonstruck poets—notably Shakespeare, Keats, Leopardi, and Dickinson defy such winnowing.

Where titles have been supplied, either to short poems without original or established titles or to extracts from long poems, they are given within square brackets—unless the title is the first line of the poem or extract, in which case it is in quotation marks.

As a whole, this collection gives rise to some intriguing questions about the creative imagination. For instance, is there an origin for moon imagery in mimetic magic? Can the old superstitious practices regarding the moon still be efficacious in charming the believer's unconscious, containing hints concerning our own psychological changes? One might even ask if the quality of a poet's imagination can be judged in relation to his interest, or lack of it, in the moon.

The last question seems absurd. Nevertheless, I suspect (as did Wallace Stevens) there are Gold poets and there are Silver poets, and they exist planets apart. Blake is a Gold poet, and so is Edith Sitwell, God knows: in Dame Edith's *Collected Poems* one counts the word "gold" 280 times, the word "golden" 94! There is not one poem in her *oeuvre* about the moon. Rather, her work stuns with its surfeit of suns, lions' heads, and honey.

Contrariwise, other poets seem equally obsessed with silver and make the moon a central symbol within their personal mythology. Such poets include Leopardi and T. E. Hulme, both of whose small bodies of poetry literally revolve about our closest celestial neighbor, as does the work of the more prolific Christina Rossetti. More recent "Silver" poets are Lindsay, Léonie Adams, Marya Zaturenska, Erica Jong, and Constance Urdang.

Then there are the extremely rare poets—Shakespeare and Emily Dickinson are two—whose work yields vast and nearly equal ores of gold and silver. That their sensibilities can embrace both *yang* and *yin*, masculine and feminine, is one measure of their greatness.

Whatever the reason for her attraction, the moon has been for most poets exactly what they make of her. In this respect she resembles the subject of my first anthology, that other changeable lady, Lewis Carroll's Alice. Such lunar variety also suggests the accuser, in one of Robert Francis's delightful *Satirical Rogue* essays, who rails, "You poets say any damn thing that comes into your head. Take the moon, for instance . . . you call it a bright penny or a beautiful woman or a ship or a balloon or a goddess or God knows what. Don't you?"

"We do," replies Francis. "The remarkable thing is that everything we say about the moon is true."

Thus, this collection embraces many imaginative transformations or "phases" of the moon, and there is necessarily some overlapping within the six designated sections: *The Orb of Love, Fables of the Moon, Lunar Masks, The Bright Side, The Dark Side,* and *After Apollo.*

The first section deals with constant and inconstant affection, lovers' attitudes changing perhaps as frequently as the shape of the moon itself. For centuries poets agreed that the night was made for love, though only good poets could say so and not be banal. It is interesting to contrast later attitudes, one poet damning the moon for exposing his stealth or ill health, another praising her for illumining his way or his soul.

The reader must account, of course, for the different names accorded the moon in this and the following sections. To A.W. she is Venus; to Baudelaire, Cynthia; to Vaughan, Etesia; and so forth. Just as the sun in nearly all myths assumes masculine identity (Hermes, Apollo, Phoebus, Helios) so the moon nearly always has been feminine—at various times addressed as Aphrodite, Venus, Vesta, Hestia, Diana, Artemis, Cynthia, Hecate, Selene, Phoebe, Virago, Elythia, Protheria, Dictinna, Proserpine, Letona, Lucinna, and Calliope among others.

So disparate have been her roles and identities that a number of poets identify the moon as the goddess with three forms—Selene in the sky, Artemis on the land, and Hecate in the underground. It is this triple guise about which Robert Graves, in *The White Goddess* (1948), has written so inspiredly. This is also the triple goddess encountered by the shepherd prince in Keats's long romance *Endymion*.

Perhaps it is the purity of the moon's light that is responsible for the early link to femininity, an association being made between the moon and the Virgin Mary. Paintings of the Middle Ages and the Renaissance portray Mary standing on a crescent pedestal. Another, albeit secular, connection is the moon's role as "governess of floods" and mistress of the tides and dews. Said to be the source of the waters of life, the moon is also connected with the menstrual cycle.

A male chauvinist might add that the moon always has been the intensely feminine sphere simply because she is the passive one, reflecting the active glory of the sun rather than generating any heat of her own. This parallels those conventional roles assigned man and woman, husband and wife, for too many unenlightened ages.

A final theory used in support of the moon's feminine nature is her changeableness. The reader will find here poems in which she

) xxvi (

is both "chaste" and "wanton," queen and whore. And like a woman during and after pregnancy, the moon's body increases and dwindles.

All these supposedly feminine attributes are exploded, however, by the first poem of the second section, *Fables of the Moon*. Here we find that beloved favorite of childhood, the *Man* in the Moon. His presence is found in a persistent minority of moon verse, from the Middle Ages to the present, when the man *in* the moon becomes the man *on* the moon. And while Sappho and other Greeks emphasized the moon's spiritual (feminine) nature, by Chaucer's time there existed legends of an earthly (male) origin. Usually the man in/on the moon was a thief, exiled there for stealing sticks; a variant offense was carrying sticks on the Sabbath. In Chaucer's *Troilus and Criseyde* he carries "a bush of thornes on his backe;" in Shakespeare's *A Midsummer-Night's Dream*, he comes with both thorns and lantern, and must "say he comes to disfigure or to present the person of moonshine." Both Chaucer's and Shakespeare's man on the moon may have been based upon the ancient legend of the stick-gathering man on the Sabbath as recorded in the Book of Numbers (15:32–36).

Other "fables" set forth in this section include the notion of the moon as a severed head (an Amazon poet), a Sargasso of earthly possessions and emotions (Pope), and a controller of the harvests (Catullus). Other traditional views are the moon as a child reared by the sun, or by a sister. The modern American poet Galway Kinnell alludes to the ancient Japanese belief that the moon is inhabited by a hare. Horace Gregory portrays her as a huntress. The section concludes with Traherne's wonderful "On Leaping Over the Moon," one of his many extended celebrations of the wonders of life and the glory of being, which quite anticipates our astronauts kangerooing in gravity-free atmosphere.

Lunar Masks contains some of the book's most brilliant imagery because poets do, indeed, "say any damn thing that comes into" their heads about her. The range is truly remarkable: to Blake the moon is a flower; to Lindsay a griffin's egg; to John Hollander a parenthesis; to Keats—and how many others?—a dying lady. (The male protagonist in Eliot's "Conversation Galante," not printed here, suggests within just three lines that the moon's a balloon, a battered lantern, and a sentimental friend!)

Some other arresting associations are Benlowe's moon as a president in a tent, Hulme's as a red-faced farmer, and Herrick's as an usurer. There is also a bit of a bestiary: the moon is a deer is a bull is a tiger is a sheep.

The sections titled *The Bright Side* and *The Dark Side* are comparatively straightforward. If the first appears thinner, it is not because there are fewer positive than negative poets (poets who, like Wordsworth, see the moon as a glory of the heavens or who like Keats felt all creation makes "a holier din/The while they feel thine airy fellowship"). It is briefer only because so many poems in all other sections of the book might have appeared there.

The Dark Side focuses on the shadow side of the moon, and hence on the individual poet's personality. Psychologists tell us that man always has associated the moon both with what is eternal and temporal, with the life-creating rhythms of the womb and the inevitable shadows of death. There always has been something unconscious, ambivalent, and enveloping about the moon and its association with the night (as well as with her secret hidden side). Since this mystery can and has been equated with the unconscious, "the rising of the moon" is the triumph of imagination and fancy over the brute and commonplace world. Man's compulsion to honor the moon is an expression of his need to pay spiritual and sexual homage to his mysterious counterpart in life, the female.

Yet the associations are more complex, as these poems illustrate. The moon's subjugation to change has fostered a belief that the moon and its dark side are sources of mental illness. In *Othello*, Shakespeare says, "It is the very error of the moon;/ She comes more nearer earth than she was wont, and makes men mad!"

The frequent changes of the moon may be compared to those of the lunatic. From the great anonymous ballad, "Tom o'Bedlam's Song," to Elinor Wylie's "Madman's Song," the link is unbroken: poets seem obsessed by a "bald and wild" moon (to quote Sylvia Plath). They would read with fascination C. G. Jung's writing on the "shadow" side of personality, which Jung claimed was both universal and personified, as in a dreamer's dream of a "demon lover," a figure from the collective unconscious.

Whether or not one subscribes to Jung's "shadow," the poems in this section support the notion of the moon as man's most potent symbol for "the other side" of existence. It is a symbol particularly appropriate for those with what psychoanalyst Anthony Storrs calls "the infantile tendency"—that trait which divides persons into black and white categories, gods and devils, virgins and witches. There are some witches in *The Dark Side*, as well as a bedlam of madmen. These poems generally follow the drift toward death. A fresh exception is the brief poem by a young American, Terry Stokes, who finds positive values in the moon's darkness.

The final section, *After Apollo*, is affirmative. And if the moon landings were, as Auden insists, merely "a phallic triumph," at least they forced the poetic sensibility to grapple with space-age technology in both human and nonhuman terms, to deal with outer weather as well as inner. Suddenly weightlessness is of as great a gravity as more earthly questions. May Swenson asks, "Dare we land upon a dream?" We did, our poets do.

The Talmud tells us, "The moon was created only to facilitate study." Of all subjects under the moon, the study of moon poems should not be overshadowed. As Richard Eberhart says in one of his poems, "To keep an eye on fables of the moon/ While feet are walking down the street/ Is not the least a man can do./ And may be most."

ROBERT PHILLIPS

Katonah, New York
July 15, 1973

I

THE ORB OF LOVE

"WE'LL GO NO MORE A-ROVING"

by George Gordon, Lord Byron

(1788–1824)

So, we'll go no more a-roving
   So late into the night,
Though the heart be still as loving,
   And the moon be still as bright.

For the sword outwears its sheath,
   And the soul wears out the breast,
And the heart must pause to breathe,
   And Love itself have rest.

Though the night was made for loving,
   And the day returns too soon,
Yet we'll go no more a-roving
   By the light of the moon.

MORNING SONG

by Sara Teasdale

(1884–1933)

A diamond of a morning
   Waked me an hour too soon;
Dawn had taken in the stars
   And left the faint white moon.

O white moon, you are lonely,
   It is the same with me,
But we have the world to roam over,
   Only the lonely are free.

THE YOUNG MAY MOON

by *Thomas Moore*

(*1779–1852*)

The young May moon is beaming, love,
The glow-worm's lamp is gleaming, love;
 How sweet to rove
 Through Morna's grove,
When the drowsy world is dreaming, love!
Then awake!—the heavens look bright, my dear,
'Tis never too late for delight, my dear;
 And the best of all ways
 To lengthen our days
Is to steal a few hours from the night, my dear!

Now all the world is sleeping, love,
But the Sage, his star-watch keeping, love,
 And I, whose star
 More glorious far
Is the eye from that casement peeping, love.
Then awake!—till rise of sun, my dear,
The Sage's glass we'll shun, my dear,
 Or in watching the flight
 Of bodies of light
He might happen to take thee for one, my dear!

WHAT COUNSEL HAS
THE HOODED MOON

by James Joyce

(1882–1941)

What counsel has the hooded moon
    Put in thy heart, my shyly sweet,
Of Love in ancient plenilune,
    Glory and stars beneath his feet—
A sage that is but kith and kin
    With the comedian Capuchin?

Believe me rather that am wise
    In disregard of the divine,
A glory kindles in those eyes,
    Trembles to starlight. Mine, O Mine!
No more be tears in moon or mist
For thee, sweet sentimentalist.

UPON VISITING HIS LADY
BY MOONLIGHT

by A.W.

(1602)

The night, say all, was made for rest;
  And so say I, but not for all:
To them the darkest nights are best
  Which give them leave asleep to fall;
    But I that seek my rest by light
    Hate sleep, and praise the clearest night.

Bright was the moon, as bright as day,
  And Venus glistered in the west,
Whose light did lead the ready way,
  That brought me to my wishéd rest:
    Then each of them increased their light
    While I enjoyed her heavenly sight.

Say, gentle dames, what moved your mind
  To shine so fair above your wont?
Would Phoebe fair Endymion find?
  Would Venus see Adonis hunt?
    No, no, you fearéd by her sight
    To lose the praise of beauty bright.

At last for shame you shrunk away,
  And thought to reave the world of light;
Then shone my dame with brighter ray,
  Than that which comes from Phoebus' sight:
    None other light but hers I praise,
    Whose nights are clearer than the days.

WITH HOW SAD STEPS

by Sir Philip Sidney

(1554–1586)

With how sad steps, O Moon, thou climbst the skies!
How silently, and with how wan a face!
What, may it be that even in heavenly place
That busy archer his sharp arrows tries?
Sure, if that long-with-love-acquainted eyes
Can judge of love, thou feel'st a lover's case:
I read it in thy looks: thy languished grace,
To me that feel the like, thy state descries.
Then even of fellowship, O Moon, tell me,
Is constant love deemed there but want of wit?
Are beauties there as proud as here they be?
Do they above love to be loved, and yet
Those lovers scorn whom that love doth possess?
Do they call virtue there ungratefulness?

TO NIGHT

by *Anonymous*

(*1593*)

O Night! O jealous Night, repugnant to my pleasures!
O Night so long desired, yet cross to my content!
There's none but only thou that can perform my pleasures,
Yet none but only thou that hindereth my intent.

Thy beams, thy spiteful beams, thy lamps that burn too brightly,
Discover all my trains and naked lay my drifts:
That night by night I hope, yet fail my purpose nightly,
Thy envious glaring gleam defeateth so my shifts.

Sweet Night! withhold thy beams, withhold them till to-morrow,
Whose joys in lack so long a hell of torments breeds;
Sweet Night, sweet gentle Night! do not prolong my sorrow:
Desire is guide to me, and love no loadstar needs.

Let sailors gaze on stars and moon so freshly shining;
Let them that miss the way be guided by the light:
I know my lady's bower, there needs no more divining,
Affection sees in dark, and love hath eyes by night.

Dame Cynthia! couch awhile, hold in thy horns from shining,
And glad not louring Night with thy too glorious rays;
But be she dim and dark, tempestuous and repining,
That in her spite my sport may work thy endless praise.

And when my will is wrought, then, Cynthia, shine—good lady!—
All other nights and days, in honour of that night,
That happy heavenly night, that night so dark and shady,
Wherein my Love had eyes that lightened my delight.

THE SHORT NIGHT

by Taniguchi Buson

(1716–1783)

Night that ends so soon:
in the ford there still remains
one sliver of the moon.

(Tr. by Harold G. Henderson)

OF THE MOON

by Charles Best

(*fl. 1602*)

Look how the pale queen of the silent night
Doth cause the ocean to attend upon her,
And he, as long as she is in his sight,
With his full tide is ready her to honour:
But when the silver wagon of the moon
Is mounted up so high he cannot follow,
The sea calls home his crystal waves to moan,
And with low ebb doth manifest his sorrow.
So you, that are the sovereign of my heart,
Have all my joys attending on your will:
My joys low ebbing when you do depart,
When you return, their tide my heart doth fill.
    So as you come, and as you do depart,
    Joys ebb and flow within my tender heart.

WHEN YON FULL MOON

by W. H. Davies

(1871–1940)

When yon full moon's with her white fleet of stars,
   And but one bird makes music in the grove;
When you and I are breathing side by side,
   Where our two bodies make one shadow, love;

Not for her beauty will I praise the moon,
   But that she lights thy purer face and throat;
The only praise I'll give the nightingale
   Is that she draws from thee a richer note.

For, blinded with thy beauty, I am filled,
   Like Saul of Tarsus, with a greater light;
When he had heard that warning voice in Heaven,
   And lost his eyes to find a deeper sight.

Come, let us sit in that deep silence then,
   Launched on love's rapids, with our passions proud,
That makes all music hollow—though the lark
   Raves in his windy heights above a cloud.

"TONIGHT I'VE WATCHED"

by Sappho

(*fl. c. 650* B.C.)

Tonight I've watched

The moon and then
the Pleides
go down

The night is now
half-gone; youth
goes; I am

in bed alone

(*Tr. by Mary Barnard*)

A YEAR PASSES

by Amy Lowell

(1874–1925)

Beyond the porcelain fence of the pleasure garden
I hear the frogs in the blue-green ricefields;
But the sword-shaped moon
Has cut my heart in two.

TO ETESIA
LOOKING FROM HER CASEMENT
AT THE FULL MOON

by Henry Vaughan

(1622–1695)

See you that beauteous Queen, which no age tames?
Her Train is Azure, set with golden flames.
My brighter fair, fix on the East your Eyes,
And view that bed of Clouds, whence she doth rise.
Above all others in that one short hour
Which most concern'd me, she had greatest pow'r.
This made my Fortunes humorous as wind,
But fix'd Affections to my constant mind.
She fed me with the tears of Starrs, and thence
I suck'd in Sorrows with their Influence.
To some in smiles, and store of light she broke:
To me in sad Eclipses still she spoke.
She bent me with the motion of her Sphere,
And made me feel, what first I did but fear.
        But when I came to Age, and had o'ergrown
Her Rules, and saw my freedom was my own,
I did reply unto the Laws of Fate,
And made my Reason, my great Advocate:
I labour'd to inherit my just right;
But then (O hear Etesia!) lest I might
Redeem my self, my unkind Starry Mother
Took my poor Heart, and gave it to another.

WHAT SEMIRAMIS SAID

(from "Poems about the Moon")

by Vachel Lindsay

(1879–1931)

The moon's a steaming chalice
Of honey and venom-wine.
A little of it sipped by night
Makes the long hours divine.
But oh, my reckless lovers,
They drain the cup and wail,
Die at my feet with shaking limbs
And tender lips all pale.
Above them in the sky it bends
Empty and grey and dread.
To-morrow night 'tis full again,
Golden, and foaming red.

THE INJURED MOON

by *Charles Baudelaire*

(*1821–1867*)

Oh Moon, discreetly worshipped by our sires,
still riding through your high blue countries, still
trailed by the shining harem of your stars,
old Cynthia, the lamp of our retreats . . .

the lovers sleep open-mouthed! When they breathe,
they show the white enamel of their teeth.
The writer breaks his teeth on his work-sheets,
the vipers couple under the hot hill.

Dressed in your yellow hood, do you pursue
your boy from night to dawn, till the sun climbs
skyward, where dim Endymion disappears?

"I see your mother, Child of these poor times,
crushed to her mirror by the heavy years.
She cunningly powders the breast that nourished you."

(Tr. by Robert Lowell)

DEAREST MAN-IN-THE-MOON

by Erica Jong

(1942–   )

ever since our lunch of cheese
& moonjuice
on the far side of the sun,
I have walked the craters of New York,
a trail of slime
ribboning between my legs,
a phosphorescent banner
which is tied to you,
a beam of moonlight
focussed on your navel,
a silver chain
from which my body dangles,
& my whole torso chiming
like sleighbells in a Russian novel.

Dearest man-in-the-moon,
I used to fear moonlight
thinking her my mother.
I used to dread nights
when the moon was full.
I used to scream
"Pull down the shade!"
because the moonface leered at me,
because I felt her mocking,
because my fear lived in me
like rats in a wheel of cheese.

You have eaten out my fear.
You have licked
the creamy inside of my moon.
You have kissed
the final crescent of my heart
& made it full.

MOON COMPASSES

by Robert Frost

(1875–1963)

I stole forth dimly in the dripping pause
Between two downpours to see what there was.
And a masked moon had spread down compass rays
To a cone mountain in the midnight haze,

As if the final estimate were hers;
And as it measured in her calipers,
The mountain stood exalted in its place.
So love will take between the hands a face. . . .

II

FABLES
OF THE MOON

THE MAN IN THE MOON

(Anon., English)

The Man in the Moon was caught in a trap
For stealing the thorns from another man's gap.
If he had gone by, and let the thorns lie,
He'd never been Man in the Moon so high.

THE CREATION OF THE MOON

(*Anonymous, Caxinua Amazon*)

The man cut his throat and left his head there.
The others went to get it.
When they got there they put the head in a sack.
Farther on the head fell out onto the ground.
They put the head back in the sack.
Farther on the head fell out again.
Around the first sack they put a second one that was thicker.
But the head fell out just the same.
It should be explained that they were taking the head
    to show to the others.
They did not put the head back in the sack.
They left it in the middle of the road.
They went away.

They crossed the river.
But the head followed them.
They climbed up a tree full of fruit
to see whether it would go past.

The head stopped at the foot of the tree
and asked them for some fruit.
So the men shook the tree.
The head went to get the fruit.
Then it asked for some more.

So the men shook the tree
so that the fruit fell into the water.
The head said it couldn't get the fruit from there.
So the men threw the fruit a long way
to make the head go a long way to get it so they could go.
While the head was getting the fruit
the men got down from the tree and went on.

The head came back and looked at the tree
and didn't see anybody

so went on rolling down the road.
The men had stopped to wait
to see whether the head would follow them.
They saw the head come rolling.

They ran.
They got to their hut they told the others that the head
was rolling after them and to shut the door.

All the huts were closed tight.
When it got there the head commanded them to open the doors.
The owners would not open them because they were afraid.

So the head started to think what it would turn into.
If it turned into water they would drink it.
If it turned into earth they would walk on it.
If it turned into a house they would live in it.
If it turned into a steer they would kill it and eat it.
If it turned into a cow they would milk it.
If it turned into wheat they would eat it.
If it turned into a bean they would cook it.
If it turned into the sun
when men were cold it would heat them.
If it turned into rain the grass would grow and
    the animals would crop it.

So it thought, and it said, "I will turn into the moon."
It called, "Open the doors, I want to get my things."
They would not open them.
The head cried. It called out, "At least give me
my two balls of twine."
They threw out the two balls of twine through a hole.
It took them and threw them into the sky.

It asked them to throw it a little stick too
to roll the thread around so it could climb up.

Then it said, "I can climb, I am going to the sky."
It started to climb.

The men opened the doors right away.
The head went on climbing.
The men shouted, "You going to the sky, head?"
It didn't answer.

As soon as it got to the Sun
it turned into the Moon.
Toward evening the Moon was white, it was beautiful.
And the men were surprised
to see that the head had turned into the Moon.

(*Tr. by W. S. Merwin*)

THE MAN IN THE MOON

(*Anonymous,*
from Gammer Gurton's Garland, *1783*)

The man in the moon came tumbling down,
    And asked his way to Norwich;
He went to the south, and burnt his mouth
    With supping hot pease-porridge.

INVOCATION

by Thomas Randolph

(1605–1635)

Come from thy palace, beauteous Queen of Greece,
Sweet Helen of the world. Rise like the morn,
Clad in the smock of night, that all the stars
May close their eyes, and then, grown blind,
Run weeping to the man i' the moon,
To borrow his dog to lead the spheres a-begging.

THE NIGHT-WALKER

by Horace Gregory

(*1898–*   )

Artemis, Artemis: there is fading
Glory in her net, in the silver
Curtain that falls from sky to street.

Above roof and cornice her face
Returns behind the silver rain;
The ancient huntress walks across night.

Sleepless, she warns and charms,
Sees the new age fallen out of the old,
New ruins where elder cities stood. Indifferent

Is she to these; she has come to warn us
That her pale life, her sterile mountains
Have outlived wars. Her arrows are unspent,

They are still falling in silver light
Above, within the city, their shadows deeper
Than any shelter on the scarred walks of earth.

She is not our being: she is wandering
Artemis who endures beyond life, she is
The light behind a cloud and has deceived
The unwary into an immoderate love of death.

[THE LOCK]

(from *The Rape of the Lock*, Canto V, 113)

by Alexander Pope

(*1688–1744*)

Some thought it mounted to the Lunar sphere,
Since all things lost on earth are treasur'd there.
There Heros' wits are kept in pond'rous vases,
And beaux', in snuff-boxes and tweezer cases.
There broken vows and death-bed alms are found,
And lovers' hearts with ends of riband bound,
The courtier's promises, and sick man's pray'rs,
The smiles of harlots, and the tears of heirs,
Cages for gnats, and chains to yoke a flea,
Dry'd butterflies, and tomes of casuistry.

THE TERROR BY NIGHT

(FRAGMENT)

by Giacomo Leopardi

(1798–1837)

ALCETAS:

> Hear me, Melissus; I will tell you a dream
> I had last night, which comes to mind again,
> Now that I see the moon. I stood at the window
> Which looks out on the field, and turned my eyes
> Up to the sky; and then, all of a sudden,
> The moon was loosened; and it seemed to me
> That coming nearer and nearer as it fell down,
> The bigger it appeared, until it tumbled
> In the middle of the field, with a crash, and was
> As big as a water-pot, and it spewed forth
> A cloud of sparks, which spluttered, just as loud
> As when you put a live coal under water
> Till it goes out. For it was in that way
> The moon, I'm telling you, in the middle of the field,
> Went out, and little by little it all turned black.
> And round about the grass went up in smoke.
> And then, looking up at the sky, I saw was left
> A kind of glimmer, or mark, or rather a hole,
> From which it had been torn, and at that sight
> I froze with terror; and don't feel easy yet.

MELISSUS:

> And well you might, indeed; for sure enough,
> The moon might tumble down into your field.

ALCETAS:

> Who knows? For don't we often see in summer
> Stars falling?

MELISSUS:
   But then, there are so many stars:
  And little harm if one or other of them
  Do fall—there's thousands left. But there is only
  This one moon in the sky, and nobody
  Has ever seen it fall, except in dreams. . . .

(Tr. by John Heath-Stubbs)

WYNKEN, BLYNKEN, AND NOD

by Eugene Field

(*1850–1895*)

Wynken, Blynken, and Nod one night
  Sailed off in a wooden shoe,—
Sailed on a river of crystal light
  Into a sea of dew.
"Where are you going, and what do you wish?"
  The old moon asked the three.
"We have come to fish for the herring fish
  That live in this beautiful sea;
Nets of silver and gold have we!"
          Said Wynken,
          Blynken,
          And Nod.

The old moon laughed and sang a song,
  As they rocked in the wooden shoe;
And the wind that sped them all night long
  Ruffled the waves of dew.
The little stars were the herring fish
  That lived in that beautiful sea—
"Now cast your nets wherever you wish,—
  Never afeard are we!"
So cried the stars to the fishermen three,
          Wynken,
          Blynken,
          And Nod.

All night long their nets they threw
  To the stars in the twinkling foam,—
Then down from the skies came the wooden shoe,
  Bringing the fishermen home:
'Twas all so pretty a sail, it seemed
  As if it could not be;

And some folk thought 'twas a dream they'd dreamed
    Of sailing that beautiful sea;
But I shall name you the fishermen three:
        Wynken,
        Blynken,
        And Nod.

Wynken and Blynken are two little eyes,
    And Nod is a little head,
And the wooden shoe that sailed the skies
    Is a wee one's trundle-bed;
So shut your eyes while Mother sings
    Of wonderful sights that be,
And you shall see the beautiful things
    As you rock in the misty sea
Where the old shoe rocked the fishermen three: —
        Wynken,
        Blynken,
        And Nod.

"THE WAVERING PLANET"

(from GILES FARNABY'S CANZONETS
TO FOWRE VOICES, 1598)

by Anon.

(16th century)

The wavering planet most unstable,
    Goddess of the waters flowing,
    That bears a sway in each thing growing
And makes my lady variable.
    Oft I seek to undermine her,
    Yet I know not where to find her.

[MEDEA CASTS A SPELL TO MAKE AESON YOUNG AGAIN]

(from "The Metamorphoses of Ovid")

by Arthur Golding

(1536?–1605?)

Before the moon should circlewise close both her horns in one
Three nights were yet as then to come. As soon as that she shone
Most full of light, and did behold the earth with fulsome face,
Medea with her hair not trussed so much as in a lace,
But flaring on her shoulders twain, and barefoot, with her gown
Ungirded, got her out of doors and wandered up and down
Alone the dead time of the night: both man, and beast, and bird
Were fast asleep: the serpents sly in trailing forward stirred
So softly that you would have thought they still asleep had been.
The moisting air was whist: no leaf ye could have moving seen.
The stars alonely fair and bright did in the welkin shine.
To which she, lifting up her hands, did thrice herself incline,
And thrice with water of the brook her hair besprinkled she:
And gasping thrice she oped her mouth: and bowing down her knee
Upon the bare hard ground, she said: 'Oh trusty time of night,
Most faithful unto privities, oh golden stars whose light
Doth jointly with the moon succeed the beams that blaze by day,
And thou, three-headed Hecate, who knowest best the way
To compass this our great attempt, and art our chiefest stay:
Ye charms and witchcrafts, and thou earth which both with
  herb and weed
Of mighty working furnishest the wizards at their need:
Ye airs and winds: ye elves of hills, of brooks, of woods alone,
Of standing lakes, and of the night, approach ye everychone.
Through help of whom (the crooked banks much wondering
  at the thing)
I have compelléd streams to run clean backward to their spring.

By charms I make the calm seas rough, and make the rough
    seas plain,
And cover all the sky with clouds, and chase them hence again.
By charms I raise and lay the winds, and burst the viper's jaw,
And from the bowels of the earth both stones and trees do draw.
Whole woods and forests I remove: I make the mountains shake,
And even the earth itself to groan and fearfully to quake.
I call up dead men from their graves: and thee, oh lightsome moon,
I darken oft, though beaten brass abate they peril soon:
Our sorcery dims the morning fair, and darks the sun at noon.
The flaming breath of fiery bulls ye quenchéd for my sake,
And causéd their unwieldy necks the bended yoke to take.
Amongst the earthbred brothers you a mortal war did set,
And brought asleep the dragon fell whose eyes were never shet;
By means wherof deceiving him that had the golden fleece
In charge to keep, you sent it thence by Jason into Greece.
Now have I need of herbs that can by virtue of their juice
To flowering prime of lusty youth old withered age reduce.
I am assured ye will it grant. For not in vain have shone
These twinkling stars, ne yet in vain this chariot all alone
By draught of dragons hither comes.' With that was fro the sky
A chariot softly glancéd down, and stayéd hard thereby.

SHOOTING AT THE MOON

by Kim Yo-sōp

(1927–   )

Every night in the town,
a boy was shooting arrows at the darkness.

His arrows flew to hit the white stars.
In the town where the meteors fell and the boy slept,
a nightmare was lit up like a lamp every night.

Once an arrow
hit the heart of the moon.

The moon shed her white blood in a stream.
The moonlight drenched the earth and the boy's dream.

The boy died with the moonlight tied round his neck.
He died in the park holding a bow in his hand.

The white moon which has lost her songs
is now lit up alone over the fountain.

(Tr. by Ko Won)

MOON ECLIPSE EXORCISM

(*Anon. Alsean poet*)

come out come out come out
the moon has been killed

> Who kills the moon? crow
> who often kills the moon? eagle
> who usually kills the moon?
>   chicken hawk
> who also kills the moon? owl
> in their numbers they assemble
> for moonkilling

come out, throw sticks at your houses
come out, turn your buckets over
spill out all the water don't let it turn
bloody yellow
from the wounding and death
of the moon

o what will become of the world, the moon
never dies without cause
only when a rich man is about to be killed
is the moon murdered

look all around the world, dance, throw your sticks,
*   help out,*
look at the moon,
>   *dark as it is now, even if it disappears*
it will come back, think of nothing
I'm going back into the house
>   *and the others went back*

(*English working by Armand Schwerner*)

"AWAKE, OH HEAVEN, FOR (LO) THE HEAVENS CONSPIRE"

(from "The Transformed Metamorphosis")

by Cyril Tourneur

(1575?–1626)

Awake, oh Heaven, for (lo) the heavens conspire;
   The silver feathered moon, and both the Bears,
Are posted down for Phlegetontike fire:
   Lo, now they are upon the azure spheres,
   (Thy soul is vexed with sense confounding fears)
Now are they mounted into Carol's wain,
With all the stars like to an arméd train.

Ay, even those stars, which for their sacred minds
   (They once terrestrial) were stellified,
With all the force of Aeol's sail—swelled winds
   And fearful thunder, vailer of earth's pride—
   Upon the lofty firmament do ride:
All with infernal concord do agree
To shake the strength of heaven's axletree.

WHEN TWO SUNS DO APPEAR

by Sir Philip Sidney

(1554–1586)

When two suns do appear,
Some say it doth betoken wonders near,
   As prince's loss or change.
Two gleaming suns of splendor like I see,
   And seeing feel in me
Of prince's heart quite lost the ruin strange.
   But now each where doth range
With ugly cloak the dark envious Night,
   Who, full of guilty spite,
Such living beams should her black seat assail,
Too weak for them our weaker sight doth vail.
   No, says fair Moon, my light
Shall bar that wrong, and though it not prevail
Like to my brother's rays, yet those I send
Hurt not the face which nothing can amend.

HOW OLD'S THE MOON?

(JAPANESE CHILDREN'S VERSE)

by Anonymous

How old's the moon?
The moon's thirteen,
Thirteen years and seven more.
The moon's still young.
It bore that child:
This other child the young moon bore.

Who'll carry the child?
Let Oman carry it.
Where, O where, is Oman gone?
Oman went to buy some tea,
To buy some oil is Oman gone.

In front of the oil-shop
Oman slipped,
Fell and spilt a quart of oil.
Then what happened?
Taro's dog
And Jiro's dog, they licked it all.

So then what happened
To those two lap-dogs?
Those two dogs have now become
One the skin
Of a tambourine,
One the skin for a big round drum.

Facing this way,
Ratta tat tat:
Facing that way, ratta tat tat.
Two dead dog-skins,
Two dead dog-skins,
Dog-skins squashed and beaten flat.
(Tr. by Graehme Wilson)

DIANAE SUMUS IN FIDE

by Catullus

(*84?–54* B.C.)

Boys and girls, we pledge allegiance
to the moon, virgin Diana,
chastity and innocence,
boys and girls all sing Diana.

O divinity, divinest
fruit of Jove, all-powerful sire,
and his Latona, your mother,
gave you birth beneath the sacred

olive tree of Delos, made you
(sing Diana) mistress of the hills,
young forests, hidden valleys
where far winding rivers
disappear in music, sing Diana.

Women in childbirth call upon your name
night goddess, queen of darkness
and false daylight. Sing Diana

who has steered the circling voyage
of the seasons into years,
bringing with her harvest time
and full granaries and rich farms:

by whatever name we call you,
(sing Diana) hear our prayers,
as years long gone you sheltered us
your sons of Romulus from harm
defend, now and forever, sing Diana!

(*Tr. by Horace Gregory*)

) 43 (

THE MOON SINGS

Anonymous verse

(from *Westminster Drollery*, 1672)

The Moon, in her pride, once glanced aside
Her eyes and espied the day;
As unto his bed, in waistcoat of red,
Fair Phoebus him led the way;
Such changes of thought, in her chastity wrought,
That thus she besought the boy,
O tarry, and marry the Starry Diana,
That will be thy Gem and Joy.

I will be as bright at noon as at night,
If that may delight the day;
Come hither and join thy glories with mine,
Together we'll shine for aye.
The night shall be noon, and every moon
As pleasant as June or May;
O tarry, and marry the Starry Diana,
That will be thy Gem and Joy.

Enamour'd of none, I live chaste and alone,
Though courted of one, some say;
And true if it were so frivolous fear
Let never my dear dismay;
I'll change my opinion, and turn my old Minion,
The Sleepy Endimion away,
O tarry, and marry the Starry Diana,
That will be thy Gem and Joy.

And but that the night should have wanted her light,
Or lovers in sight should play,
Or Phoebus should shame to bestow such a dame
(With a dow'r of his flame) on a boy,
Or day should appear, eternally here,
And night otherwhere, the day
Had tarry'd and marry'd the starry'd Diana,
And she been his Gem and Joy.

PROMONTORY MOON

by Galway Kinnell

(*1927–*)

The moon: she shakes off her cloaks,
Her rings of mist and circle of blurred light,
And shines without chemistry or heat
Upon us. Milky blue in her influence
The sea rises dabbing at the tiers of rock.
A few shadowy rabbits dash feinting
Over the grass and paths. In sunlight
Men will sprawl generating on the grass;
But the rabbits ask nothing of the moon,
And run at midnight for delight alone.

Half rabbits, half rabbits' shadows,
They are like the night roistering fairies
For whom as children we set banquets
In the dusk, of bits of bread and honey,
That we explored for in the dawn and found
Untouched, the one trace of fairies being
The dew glistening on the moss and grass
At daybreak, which they shed for sorrow
Their weightless bodies have no appetite,
Being woven by the night of moonlight.

The sun makes the grass increase, feeding
The things it can corrupt. The moon
Holds her purer watches on the night,
Mirroring on that fairest time of day
Only the subtlest miracles of light;
And that within ourselves too straight to bend
In agonies of death and birth—as now
The blue-white sea swirls at the moonbeams
And keeps on winding on the shining clew—
Dissolves at her touch and is weaved anew.

[TO VESTA]

(from "The Ghost of Lucrece")

by Thomas Middleton

(*1580–1627*)

Saint Vesta! Oh thou sanctifying saint,
That lends a beam unto the clearest sun,
Which else within his fiery course would faint,
And end his race ere he had half begun,
Making the world believe his power were done,
   His oil burnt out, his lamp returned to slime,
   His fires extinguished by the breath of time;

Oh thou, the pearl that hangs on Juno's brow
Like to the moon, the massy pearl of night;
Thou jewel in the ear of Jove to show
The pride of love, the purity of light;
Thou Atlas of both worlds; umpire of right;
   Thou haven of heaven; th' assigner of each sign;
   Sanctity's saint; Divinity's divine;

Oh thou, the silver taper of the moon
Set in an alabaster candlestick
That by the bed of heaven at afternoon
Stands like a lily (which fair virgins pick
To match it with the lily of their cheek);
   Thou lily lamb; thou crystal-feathered dove
   That nestles in the palace of thy Jove;

Oh, touch my veins again, thou blood divine!
Oh, feed my spirit, thou food angelical,
And all chaste functions with my soul combine!
Colour my ghost with chastity, whose all
Feeds fat lean Death and Time in general!
   Come silver dove, heaven's alabaster nun,
   I'll hug thee more than ever I have done.

HYMN TO ARTEMIS, THE DESTROYER

by Marya Zaturenska

(*1902–*   )

Gray-eyed huntress in whose hair
The crescent moon unquiet lies,
Descending from your mountain stair
Spare the frightened hart—O spare
The warm heart that atrophies.

Under your moon-clouded gaze
The pearl-tipped, star-bright bow we see,
Winging into sterile days,
Days devoid of hope and praise
Never fruitful, wide, or free.

Ah your blazing, stinging, arrow—
Chastity's too rigid flame!
The freezing dove, the starving sparrow
Flying, fall, and call your name.

Now from your cold mountain top
You descend—the harried deer
Spill their lifeblood, drop by drop:
All life's glowing motions stop
In an ecstasy of fear.

But the escaping soul that flies
Into warmer courts of air,
Remembering your moon-shaded eyes
And your heaven-breathing hair,
Ever for your presence sighs.

TO THE MOON

by Percy Bysshe Shelley

(*1792–1822*)

Art thou pale for weariness
Of climbing heaven and gazing on the earth,
 Wandering companionless
Among the stars that have a different birth,
And ever changing, like a joyless eye
That finds no object worth its constancy?

ON LEAPING OVER THE MOON

by *Thomas Traherne*

(*1637?–1674?*)

I saw new worlds beneath the water lie,
 New people; and another sky
  And sun, which seen by day
  Might things more clear display.
   Just such another
   Of late my brother
Did in his travel see, and saw by night
 A much more strange and wondrous sight;
Nor could the world exhibit such another
 So great a sight, but in a brother.

Adventure strange! No such in story we
 New or old, true or feignéd, see.
  On earth he seemed to move,
  Yet heaven went above;
   Up in the skies
   His body flies
In open, visible, yet magic, sort;
 As he along the way did sport,
Like Icarus over the flood he soars
 Without the help of wing or oars.

As he went tripping o'er the king's highway,
 A little pearly river lay,
  O'er which, without a wing
  Or oar, he dared to swim,
   Swim through the air
   On body fair;
He would not trust Icarian wings,
 Lest they should prove deceitful things;
For had he fall'n, it had been wondrous high,
 Not from, but from above, the sky.

He might have dropped through that thin element
  Into a fathomless descent;
    Unto the nether sky
    That did beneath him lie,
      And there might tell
      What wonders dwell
On earth above. Yet doth he briskly runs
  And, bold, the danger overcomes:
Who, as he leapt, with joy related soon
  How *happy he* o'erleapt the moon.

What wondrous things upon the earth are done
  Beneath, and yet above, the sun?
    Deeds all appear again
    In higher spheres; remain
      In clouds as yet,
      But there they get
Another light, and in another way
  Themselves to us *above* display.
The skies themselves this earthly globe surround;
  We're even here within them found.

On heav'nly ground within the skies we walk,
  And in this middle center talk:
    Did we but wisely move,
    On earth in heav'n above,
      We then should be
      Exalted high
Above the sky; from whence whoever falls,
  Through a long dismal precipice,
Sinks to the deep abyss where Satan crawls,
  Where horrid death and déspair lies.

As much as others thought themselves to lie
  Beneath the moon, so much more high
    Himself he thought to fly
    Above the starry sky,
      As *that* he spied
      Below the tide.

Thus did he yield me in the shady night
   A wondrous and instructive light,
Which taught me that under our feet there is
   As o'er our heads, a place of bliss.

III

LUNAR MASKS

THE MOONSHEEP

by *Christian Morgenstern*

(1871–1914)

The moonsheep stands in the open plain,
waiting, waiting, for the shear's refrain.
         The moonsheep.

The moonsheep pulls a single blade
and then goes home to his alpine glade.
         The moonsheep.

The moonsheep, dreaming, does with himself converse:
"I am the dark space of the universe."
         The moonsheep.

The moonsheep in the morn lies dead.
His body's white, the sun is red.
         The moonsheep.

(Tr. by E. M. Valk)

MOON TIGER

by Denise Levertov

(1923–   )

The moon tiger.
In the room, here.
It came in, it is
prowling sleekly
under and over
the twin beds.
See its small head,
silver smooth,
hear the pad of its
large feet. Look,
its white stripes
in the light that slid
through the jalousies.
It is sniffing our
clothes, its cold nose
nudges our bodies.
The beds are narrow,
but I'm coming in with you.

IMAGES

by Alastair Campbell

(*1926–*   )

The moon
    is a white
          bull
    deliciously
          stepping
     on velvet

THE CRESCENT MOON

(Riddle, Anonymous)

In Mornigan's park there is a deer,
Silver horns and golden ear,
Neither fish, flesh, feather nor bone,
In Mornigan's park she walks alone.

YET GENTLE WILL THE GRIFFIN BE

(What Grandpa Told the Children)

(from "Poems about the Moon")

by Vachel Lindsay

(1879–1931)

The moon? It is a griffin's egg,
Hatching to-morrow night.
And how the little boys will watch
With shouting and delight
To see him break the shell and stretch
And creep across the sky.
The boys will laugh. The little girls,
I fear, may hide and cry.
Yet gentle will the griffin be,
Most decorous and fat,
And walk up to the milky way
And lap it like a cat.

WHO KNOWS

by e. e. cummings

(1894–1962)

who knows if the moon's
a balloon,coming out of a keen city
in the sky—filled with pretty people?
(and if you and i should

get into it,if they
should take me and take you into their balloon,
why then
we'd go up higher with all the pretty people

than houses and steeples and clouds:
go sailing
away and away sailing into a keen
city where nobody's ever visited,where

always
            it's
                    Spring) and everyone's
in love and flowers pick themselves

SONG OF AMERGIN

(Ancient Celtic calendar-alphabet)

I am a stag: *of seven tines,*
I am a flood: *across a plain,*
I am a wind: *on a deep lake,*
I am a tear: *the Sun lets fall,*
I am a hawk: *above the cliff,*
I am a thorn: *beneath the nail,*
I am a wonder: *among flowers,*
I am a wizard: *who but I*
Sets the cool head aflame with smoke?

I am a spear: *that roars for blood,*
I am a salmon: *in a pool,*
I am a lure: *from paradise,*
I am a hill: *where poets walk,*
I am a boar: *renowned and red,*
I am a breaker: *threatening doom,*
I am a tide: *that drags to death,*
I am an infant: *who but I*
Peeps from the unhewn dolmen arch?

I am the womb: *of every holt,*
I am the blaze: *on every hill,*
I am the queen: *of every hive,*
I am the shield: *for every head,*
I am the grave: *of every hope.*

(Text restored by Robert Graves)

) 61 (

[THE MOON]

(from "The Night")

by William Blake

(1757–1827)

The moon like a flower
In heaven's high bower,
With silent delight
Sits and smiles on the night.

AUTUMN

by T. E. Hulme

(*1883–1917*)

A touch of cold in the Autumn night
I walked abroad,
And saw the ruddy moon lean over a hedge
Like a red-faced farmer.
I did not stop to speak, but nodded;
And round about were the wistful stars
With white faces like town children.

THE ONE-EYED BRIDEGROOM

by Constance Urdang

(*1922–*   )

I have said I will marry the moon,
Little husband of all women,
The son of the serpent,
The one-eyed bridegroom.

For in the keen edge of his sickle,
In his flood-tide,
In the mirror which is himself,
My secrets are hidden.

I marry you in the name of Eve,
Who is the face within the circle;
In the sign of the hare with three legs.
Our first daughter will be a cat, and see in the dark.

Eye of the world, milky, blind, inward-turning eye,
In the dark of the moon, behold! the spouse.

UPON MOON

by Robert Herrick

(1591–1674)

Moon is an Usurer, whose gain,
Seldome or never, knows a wain,
Onely Moons conscience, we confesse,
That ebs from pittie lesse and lesse.

[CYNTHIA]

(from *Theophila*, 1625)

by Edward Benlowes

(*1603–1676*)

So Cynthia seems Star chamber's president,
    With crescent splendour from Sol lent,
Rallying her starry group to guard her glittering tent.

Pearléd dews and stars. Yet earth's shade shuts up soon
    Her shop of beams; whose cone doth run
'Bove th' horned moon, beneath the golden-tresséd sun.

Wh'on sky, clouds, seas, earth, rocks doth rays disperse,
    Stars, rainbows, pearls, fruits, diamonds pierce;
The world's eye, source of light, soul of the universe.

Who glows like carbuncles, when winged hours
    Dandle the infant morn, which scours
Dame Luna, with her twinkling spies, from azure tow'rs.

[IS THE MOON TIRED?]

(from "Sing-Song")

by *Christina Rossetti*

(*1830–1894*)

Is the moon tired? she looks so pale
Within her misty veil:
She scales the sky from east to west,
And takes no rest.

Before the coming of the night
The moon shows papery white;
Before the dawning of the day
She fades away.

MOON'S ENDING

by Sara Teasdale

(1884–1933)

Moon, worn thin to the width of a quill,
    In the dawn clouds flying,
How good to go, light into light, and still
    Giving light, dying.

TO AN OLD LADY

by *William Empson*

(*1906–*   )

Ripeness is all; her in her cooling planet
Revere; do not presume to think her wasted.
Project her no projectile, plan nor man it;
Gods cool in turn, by the sun long outlasted.

Our earth alone given no name of god
Gives, too, no hold for such a leap to aid her;
Landing, you break some palace and seem odd;
Bees sting their need, the keeper's queen invader.

No, to your telescope; spy out the land;
Watch while her ritual is still to see,
Still stand her temples emptying in the sand
Whose waves o'erthrew their crumbled tracery;

Still stand uncalled-on her soul's appanage;
Much social detail whose successor fades,
Wit used to run a house and to play Bridge,
And tragic fervour, to dismiss her maids.

Years her precession do not throw from gear.
She reads a compass certain of her pole;
Confident, finds no confines on her sphere,
Whose failing crops are in her sole control.

Stars how much further from me fill my night.
Strange that she too should be inaccessible,
Who shares my sun. He curtains her from sight,
And but in darkness is she visible.

WASHED IN SILVER

by James Stephens

(1882–1950)

Gleaming in silver are the hills!
Blazing in silver is the sea!

And a silvery radiance spills
Where the moon drives royally!

Clad in silver tissue, I
March magnificently by!

WIND AND SILVER

by Amy Lowell

(*1874–1925*)

Greatly shining,
The Autumn moon floats in the thin sky;
And the fish-ponds shake their backs and
    flash their dragon scales
As she passes over them.

[O LADY MOON]

(from "Sing-Song")

by Christina Rossetti

(1830–1894)

O Lady Moon, your horns point toward the east;
Shine, be increased:
O Lady Moon, your horns point toward the west;
Wane, be at rest.

LAST QUARTER

by John Hollander

(1929–   )

No new moon in its arms,
and yet, and yet . . .

```
                                              When
                                        parentheses
                                      appear to be
                                    opening then
                                  beware of an
                                ending Never
                              misread such
                            signs as the
                          bold crescive
                        Cs of becoming
                      or of initials
                    curving toward
                  the words like
                Come Clear Cup
              Changes Comedy
            Crystal Create
          or even Crowns
          Their openings
          stand only for
          closings As if
          our cupped left
          hands held out
          sickle-like to
          cradle a round
          towers bulbous
          copper top cut
          some blue some
          room some hope
          out of the skys
           fierce surplus
           so these C-like
            marks close up
            But C-creatures
             grow yea truly
              behind and yet
               beyond limits
                So unrealities
                 conclude in an
                  eclipse of old
                   moonlights by
                    the darknesses
                     of origin Here
                      where the horn
                       of light thins
                        out into what
                         is almost gone
                          or lost a new
                           form starts as
                            a part of life
                             begins
```

THE NEW MOON

by Kobayashi Issa

(1763–1827)

Just three days old,
    the moon, and it's all warped and bent!
    How keen the cold!

(Tr. by Harold G. Henderson)

EVENING

by Richard Aldington

(1892–1962)

The chimneys, rank on rank,
Cut the clear sky;
The Moon
With a rag of gauze about her loins
Poses among them, an awkward Venus—
And here am I looking wantonly at her
Over the kitchen sink.

MOONRISE

by D. H. Lawrence

(1885–1930)

And who has seen the moon, who has not seen
Her rise from out the chamber of the deep,
Flushed and grand and naked, as from the chamber
Of finished bridegroom, seen her rise and throw
Confession of delight upon the wave,
Littering the waves with her own superscription
Of bliss, till all her lambent beauty shakes toward us
Spread out and known at last, and we are sure
That beauty is a thing beyond the grave,
That perfect, bright experience never falls
To nothingness, and time will dim the moon
Sooner than our full consummation here
In this odd life will tarnish or pass away.

MOONRISE

by Gerard Manley Hopkins

(1844–1889)

I awoke in the Midsummer not-to-call night, in the white
    and the walk of the morning:
The moon, dwindled and thinned to the fringe of a fingernail
    held to the candle,
Or paring of paradisaical fruit, lovely in waning but lustreless,
Stepped from the stool, drew back from the barrow, of dark
    Maenefa the mountain;
A cusp still clasped him, a fluke yet fanged him, entangled him,
    not quit utterly.
This was the prized, the desirable sight, unsought, presented so
    easily,
Parted me leaf and leaf, divided me, eyelid and eyelid of slumber.

[PHASES OF THE MOON]

(from "One Word More")

by Robert Browning

(1812–1889)

Lo, the moon's self!
Here in London, yonder late in Florence,
Still we find her face, the thrice-transfigured.
Curving on a sky imbrued with colour,
Drifted over Fiesole by twilight,
Came she, our new crescent of a hair's-breadth.
Full she flared it, lamping Samminiato,
Rounder 'twixt the cypresses and rounder,
Perfect, till the nightingales applauded.
Now, a piece of her old self, impoverished,
Hard to greet, she traverses the houseroofs,
Hurries with unhandsome thrift of silver,
Goes dispiritedly, glad to finish.

[ORBED MAIDEN]

(from *The Cloud*, 1818)

by Percy Bysshe Shelley

(*1792–1828*)

That orbéd maiden with white fire laden,
   Whom mortals call the Moon,
Glides glimmering o'er my fleece-like floor,
   By the midnight breezes strewn;
And wherever the beat of her unseen feet,
   Which only the angels hear,
May have broken the woof of my tent's thin roof,
   The stars peep behind her and peer.
And I laugh to see them whirl and flee
   Like a swarm of golden bees,
When I widen the rent in my wind-built tent,—
   Till the calm rivers, lakes, and seas,
Like strips of the sky fallen through me on high,
   Are each paved with the moon and these.

"THE MOON WAS BUT A CHIN OF GOLD"

by Emily Dickinson

(*1820–1886*)

The Moon was but a Chin of Gold
A Night or two ago—
And now she turns Her perfect Face
Upon the World below—

Her Forehead is of Amplest Blonde—
Her Cheek—a Beryl hewn—
Her Eye unto the Summer Dew
The likest I have known—

Her Lips of Amber never part—
But what must be the smile
Upon Her Friend she could confer
Were such Her Silver Will—

And what a privilege to be
But the remotest Star—
For Certainty She take Her Way
Beside Your Palace Door—

Her Bonnet is the Firmament—
The Universe—Her Shoe—
The Stars—the Trinkets at Her Belt—
Her Dimities—of Blue—

"THETIS IS THE MOON-GODDESS"

(from *Helen in Egypt*, Leuké Book Seven, I)

H.D.

(1886–1961)

Thetis is the Moon-goddess
and can change her shape,
she is Selene, is Artemis;

she is the Moon, her sphere
is remote, white, near,
is *Leuké*, is marble and snow,

is here; this is Leuké,
a-drift, a shell but held
to its central pole

or its orbit;
this is the white island,
this is the hollow shell,

this is the ship a-drift,
this is the ship at rest,
let me stay here;

is it Death to know
this immaculate purity,
security?

THE FREEDOM OF THE MOON

by Robert Frost

(1865–1963)

I've tried the new moon tilted in the air
Above a hazy tree-and-farmhouse cluster
As you might try a jewel in your hair.
I've tried it fine with little breadth of luster,
Alone, or in one ornament combining
With one first-water star almost as shining.

I put it shining anywhere I please.
By walking slowly on some evening later
I've pulled it from a crate of crooked trees,
And brought it over glossy water, greater,
And dropped it in, and seen the image wallow,
The color run, all sorts of wonder follow.

BECAUSE THE THREE MOIRAI
HAVE BECOME THE THREE MARIES,
OR FAITH, HOPE, AND CHARITY

by Constance Urdang

(*1922–*   )

Moon that is a cow, being horned like her,
Moon that is a panther, rapacious of light,
Moon that is a she-bear, a lioness,
Three-headed hound of the moon,
Moon-muse, mother, fountain that rises and falls,
Your daughters do not forget you.
You make their weather. Their blood
Ebbs and flows like the tides you make.

On one cusp of your crescent, the Black Virgin,
Veiled compassionate daughter, mediatrix, lover of men;
The Mermaid on the other, false siren, half fish,
Half woman, born of the sea, sea-water in
Her veins, salty and cold as the sea; they are
Your children, these two; forget them not.

I standing on your crescent, madonna, moon,
Old woman that never dies, being perpetually
Renewed, made nothing again, made small again,
Waxing again, going through it all over again,
I would lift up my song, bark, howl, bay to you;
I would say to you, remember me, beloved 3-headed nurse,
I have swallowed your milk, you wiped me and wrapped me;
Beautiful motherly monster, watch over me still.

IV

THE BRIGHT SIDE

THE NEW MOON

by Sara Teasdale

(1884–1933)

Day, you have bruised and beaten me,
As rain beats down the bright, proud sea,
Beaten my body, bruised my soul,
Left me nothing lovely or whole—
Yet I have wrested a gift from you,
Day that dies in dusky blue:

For suddenly over the factories
I saw a moon in the cloudy seas—
A wisp of beauty all alone
    In a world as hard and gray as stone—
Oh who could be bitter and want to die
When a maiden moon wakes up in the sky?

HYMN TO DIANA

(from "Cynthia's Revels")

by Ben Jonson

(1572–1637)

Queene and Huntresse, chaste and faire,
Now the sunne is laid to sleepe,
Seated, in thy silver chaire,
State in wonted manner keepe;
    Hesperus intreats thy light,
    Goddesse excellently bright.

Earth, let not thy envious shade
Dare itself to interpose;
Cynthia's shining orbe was made
Heaven to cleere, when day did close;
    Blesse us then with wishéd sight,
    Goddesse excellently bright.

Lay thy bow of pearle apart,
And thy crystall-shining quiver;
Give unto the flying hart
Space to breathe, how short soever:
    Thou that mak'st a day of night
    Goddesse excellently bright.

WELCOME TO THE MOON

(*Anonymous, from the Gaelic*)

Welcome, precious stone of the night,
Delight of the skies, precious stone of the night,
Mother of stars, precious stone of the night,
Child reared by the sun, precious stone of the night,
Excellency of stars, precious stone of the night.

CYNTHIA, BECAUSE YOUR HORNS
LOOK DIVERSE WAYS

by Fulke Greville, Lord Brooke

(*1554–1628*)

Cynthia, because your horns look diverse ways,
Now darkened to the East, now to the West;
Then at full glory once in thirty days,
Sense doth believe that change is nature's rest.

Poor earth, that dare presume to judge the sky;
Cynthia is ever round, and never varies;
Shadows and distance do abuse the eye,
And in abuséd sense, truth oft miscarries:
> Yet who this language to the People speaks,
> Opinion's empire, sense's idol breaks.

"I GAZED UPON
THE CLOUDLESS MOON"

by Emily Brontë

(1818–1848)

I gazed upon the cloudless moon,
And loved her all the night,
Till morning came and radiant noon,
And I forgot her light—

No, not forget—eternally
Remains its memory dear;
But could the day seem dark to me
Because the night was fair?

SONNET

by King James I

(*1566–1625*)

The azured vault, the crystal circles bright,
The gleaming fiery torches powdered there;
The changing round, the shining beamy light,
The sad and bearded fires, the monsters fair;
The prodigies appearing in the air;
The rearding thunders and the blustering winds;
The fowls in hue and shape and nature rare,
The pretty notes that winged musicians finds;
In earth, the savoury flowers, the metalled minds,
The wholesome herbs, the hautie pleasant trees,
The silver streams, the beasts of sundry kinds,
The bounded roars and fishes of the seas,—
    All these, for teaching man, the Lord did frame
    To do his will whose glory shines in thame.

MOON, SON OF HEAVEN
by Gary Snyder
(1930–   )

(Tr. from Miyazawa Kenji)

When I was a child
in all sorts of magazines and newspapers
    —how many—photographs of the moon;
face scarred by jagged craters.
I clearly saw that the sun light strikes it.
later I learned it's terribly cold
        and no air.
maybe three times I saw it eclipsed—
the earth's shadow
slipped over it, clearly.
next, that it probably broke off from earth.
and last, a fellow I met during rice planting
    from the Morioka meteorological observatory
    once showed me that heavenly body through
    a something-mm little telescope
    and explained how its orbit and motions
accord with a simple formula.

However. ah,
for me in the end there's no obstacle
to reverently titling that heavenly body
Emperor Moon.
if someone says
    man is his body
    that's a mistake.
    and if someone says
    man is body and mind
    that too is an error
    and if one says man is mind,
    still it's wrong.
so—I—
hail the moon as Emperor Moon.
this is not mere personification.

HAIKU

by Taniguchi Buson

(1715–1783)

The halo of the moon—
    Is it not the scent of plum-blossoms
    Rising up to heaven?

TO THE MOON

by Charlotte Smith

(1749–1806)

Queen of the silver bow!—by thy pale beam,
Alone and pensive, I delight to stray,
And watch thy shadow trembling in the stream,
Or mark the floating clouds that cross thy way.
And while I gaze, thy mild and placid light
Sheds a soft calm upon my troubled breast;
And oft I think—fair planet of the night—
That in thy orb, the wretched may have rest:
The sufferers of the earth perhaps may go,
Released by Death—to thy benignant sphere,
And the sad children of Despair and Woe
Forget, in thee, their cup of sorrow here.
Oh! that I soon may reach thy world serene,
Poor wearied pilgrim—in this toiling scene!

"THE HALF MOON SHOWS
A FACE OF PLAINTIVE SWEETNESS"

by Christina Rossetti

(*1830–1894*)

The half moon shows a face of plaintive sweetness
    Ready and poised to wax or wane;
A fire of pale desire in incompleteness,
    Tending to pleasure or to pain: —
Lo, while we gaze she rolleth on in fleetness
    To perfect loss or perfect gain.
Half bitterness we know, we know half sweetness;
    This world is all on wax, on wane:
When shall completeness round time's incompleteness,
    Fulfilling joy, fulfilling pain? —
Lo, while we ask, life rolleth on in fleetness
    To finished loss or finished gain.

A NIGHT-PIECE

by *William Wordsworth*

(*1770–1850*)

—The sky is overcast
With a continuous cloud of texture close,
Heavy and wan, all whitened by the Moon,
Which through that veil is indistinctly seen,
A dull, contracted circle, yielding light
So feebly spread that not a shadow falls,
Chequering the ground—from rock, plant, tree, or tower.
At length a pleasant instantaneous gleam
Startles the pensive traveller while he treads
His lonesome path, with unobserving eye
Bent earthwards; he looks up—the clouds are split
Asunder,—and above his head he sees
The clear Moon, and the glory of the heavens.
There, in a black-blue vault she sails along,
Followed by multitudes of stars, that, small
And sharp, and bright, along the dark abyss
Drive as she drives: how fast they wheel away,
Yet vanish not!—the wind is in the tree,
But they are silent;—still they roll along
Immeasurably distant; and the vault,
Built round by those white clouds, enormous clouds,
Still deepens its unfathomable depth.
At length the Vision closes; and the mind,
Not undisturbed by the delight it feels,
Which slowly settles into peaceful calm,
Is left to muse upon the solemn scene.

PARTIAL ECLIPSE

by W. D. Snodgrass

(1926–   )

*Last night's eclipse, 99 per-
cent complete, seemed at times
to be total because of light
mists and low-hanging clouds.*
—RADIO NEWS REPORT

Once we'd packed up your clothes
    It was something to talk about:
The full moon, how it rose
    Red, went pale, and went out

As that slow shadow crossed—
    The way Time might erase
Its blackboard: one cheek lost,
    The eyes, most of the face

Hovering dim as a ghost,
    As the dark print of some light
That seared the eyes, almost,
    Lives on in the lids, clenched tight.

Yet still one brilliant sliver
    Stayed, thin as a fingernail;
Then that went vague, would shiver,
    Till even it would fail

And the sky blank, bereft.
    But no; the mists drifted on;
Something, something was left.
    Next morning you had gone.

HEAVEN'S QUEENE

by Sir Walter Raleigh

(1552–1618)

In heaven Queene is she among the spheares,
In ay she Mistress like makes all things pure,
Eternitie in hir of chaunge she beares,
She beauty is, by hir the faire endure.

Time weares hir not, she doth his chariot guide,
Mortalitie belowe hir orbe is plaste,
By hir the vertue of the starrs downe slide,
In his is vertues perfect image cast.

    A knowledge pure it is hir worth to kno,
    With Circes let them dwell that think not so.

[THE MOON AND THE NIGHTINGALE]

(from *Paradise Lost*, IV, ll. 598–609)

by *John Milton*

(*1608–1674*)

Now came still Ev'ning on, and Twilight gray
Had in her sober Livery all things clad;
Silence accompanied, for Beast and Bird,
They to thir grassy Couch, these to thir Nests,
Were slunk, all but the wakeful Nightingale;
She all night long her amorous descant sung;
Silence was pleas'd: now glow'd the Firmament
With living Sapphires: Hesperus that led
The starry Host, rode brightest, till the Moon
Rising in clouded Majesty, at length
Apparent Queen unveil'd her peerless light,
And o'er the dark her Silver Mantle threw.

[AS WHEN THE MOON HATH COMFORTED THE NIGHT]

(from "The Conspiracy of Charles, Duke of Byron, 1608")

by George Chapman

(1559?–1634)

Laffin:
As when the moon hath comforted the night,
And set the world in silver of her light,
The planets, asterisms, and whole State of Heaven
In beams of gold, descending; all the winds
Bound up in caves, charged not to drive abroad
Their cloudy heads; and universal peace
(Proclaimed in silence) of the quiet earth:
Soon as her hot and dry fumes are let loose,
Storms and clouds mixing suddenly put out
The eyes of all these glories; the creation
Turned into chaos; and we then desire
For all our joy of life the death of sleep.
So, when the glories of our lives (men's loves,
Clear consciences, our fames and loyalties)
That did us worthy comfort are eclipsed,
Grief and disgrace invade us; and for all
Our night of life besides, our misery craves
Dark earth would ope and hide us in our graves.

"I WATCHED THE MOON AROUND THE HOUSE"

by Emily Dickinson

(1820–1886)

I watched the Moon around the House
Until upon a Pane—
She stopped—a Traveller's privilege—for Rest—
And there upon

I gazed—as at a stranger—
The Lady in the Town
Doth think no incivility
To lift her Glass—upon—

But never Stranger justified
The Curiosity
Like Mine—for not a Foot—nor Hand—
Nor Formula—had she—

But like a Head—a Guillotine
Slid carelessly away—
Did independent, Amber—
Sustain her in the sky—

Or like a Stemless Flower—
Upheld in rolling Air
By finer Gravitations—
Than bind Philosopher—

No Hunger—had she—nor an Inn—
Her Toilette—to suffice—
Nor Avocation—nor Concern
For little Mysteries

As harass us—like Life—and Death—
And Afterwards—or Nay—
But seemed engrossed to Absolute—
With shining—and the Sky—

The privilege to scrutinize
Was scarce upon my Eyes
When, with a Silver practise—
She vaulted out of Gaze—

And next—I met her on a Cloud—
Myself too far below
To follow her superior Road—
Or its advantage—Blue—

"ARE THEN REGALITIES ALL GILDED MASKS?"

(from "Endymion," Book III 1. 22–71)

by John Keats

(*1795–1821*)

Are then regalities all gilded masks?
No, there are throned seats unscalable
But by a patient wing, a constant spell,
Or by ethereal things that, unconfin'd,
Can make a ladder of the eternal wind,
And poize about in cloudy thunder-tents
To watch the abysm-birth of elements.
Aye, 'bove the withering of old-lipp'd Fate
A thousand Powers keep religious state,
In water, fiery realm, and airy bourne;
And, silent as a consecrated urn,
Hold sphery sessions for a season due.
Yet few of these far majesties, ah, few!
Have bared their operations to this globe—
Few, who with gorgeous pageantry enrobe
Our piece of heaven—whose benevolence
Shakes hand with our own Ceres; every sense
Filling with spiritual sweets to plenitude,
As bees gorge full their cells. And, by the feud
'Twixt Nothing and Creation, I here swear,
Eterne Apollo! that thy Sister fair
Is of all these the gentlier-mightiest.
When thy gold breath is misting in the west,
She unobserved steals unto her throne,
And there she sits most meek and most alone;
As if she had not pomp subservient;
As if thine eye, high Poet! was not bent
Towards her with the Muses in thine heart;
As if the ministring stars kept not apart,

Waiting for silver-footed messages.
O Moon! the oldest shades 'mong oldest trees
Feel palpitations when thou lookest in:
O Moon! old boughs lisp forth a holier din
The while they feel thine airy fellowship.
Thou dost bless every where, with silver lip
Kissing dead things to life. The sleeping kine,
Couch'd in thy brightness, dream of fields divine:
Innumerable mountains rise, and rise,
Ambitious for the hallowing of thine eyes;
And yet thy benediction passeth not
One obscure hiding-place, one little spot
Where pleasure may be sent: the nested wren
Has thy fair face within its tranquil ken,
And from beneath a sheltering ivy leaf
Takes glimpses of thee; thou art a relief
To the poor patient oyster, where it sleeps
Within its pearly house.—The mighty deeps,
The monstrous sea is thine—the myriad sea!
O Moon! far-spooming Ocean bows to thee,
And Tellus feels his forehead's cumbrous load.

a finger points to the moon

by R. D. Laing

(1927–   )

a finger points to the moon

Put the expression
     a finger points to the moon, in brackets
     (a finger points to the moon)
The statement:
     'A finger points to the moon is in brackets'
is an attempt to say that all that is in the bracket
     (   )
is, as to that which is not in the bracket,
what a finger is to the moon

Put all possible expressions in brackets
Put all possible forms in brackets
and put the brackets in brackets

Every expression, and every form,
is to what is expressionless and formless
what a finger is to the moon
all expressions and all forms
point to the expressionless and formless

the proposition
     'All forms point to the formless'
is itself a formal proposition

TO THE MOON

by Johann Wolfgang Goethe

(1749–1842)

Flooding with a brilliant mist
Valley, bush and tree,
You release me. Oh for once
Heart and soul I'm free!

Easy on the region round
Goes your wider gaze,
Like a friend's indulgent eye
Measuring my days.

Every echo from the past,
Glum or gaudy mood,
Haunts me—weighing bliss and pain
In the solitude.

River, flow and flow away;
Pleasure's dead to me:
Gone the laughing kisses, gone
Lips and loyalty.

All in my possession once!
Such a treasure yet
Any man would pitch in pain
Rather than forget.

Water, rush along the pass,
Never lag at ease;
Rush, and rustle to my song
Changing melodies,

How in dark December you
Roll amok in flood;
Curling, in the gala May,
Under branch and bud.

) 107 (

Happy man, that rancor-free
Shows the world his door;
One companion by—and both
In a glow before

Something never guessed by men
Or rejected quite:
Which, in mazes of the breast,
Wanders in the night.

(*Tr. by John Frederick Nims*)

V

THE DARK SIDE

THE CRAZED MOON

by W. B. Yeats

(1865–1939)

Crazed through much child-bearing
The moon is staggering in the sky;
Moon-struck by the despairing
Glances of her wandering eye
We grope, and grope in vain,
For children born of her pain.

Children dazed or dead!
When she in all her virginal pride
First trod on the mountain's head
What stir ran through the countryside
Where every foot obeyed her glance!
What manhood led the dance!

Fly-catchers of the moon,
Our hands are blenched, our fingers seem
But slender needles of bone;
Blenched by that malicious dream
They are spread wide that each
May rend what comes in reach.

THE WANING MOON

by Percy Bysshe Shelley

(1792–1822)

And, like a dying lady lean and pale,
Who totters forth, wrapped in gauzy veil,
Out of her chamber, led by the insane
And feeble wanderings of her fading brain,
The moon arose up in the murky East,
A white and shapeless mass.

MOONLIGHT

by Guillaume Apollinaire

(1880–1918)

The honeyflowing moon is on every madman's tongue
Tonight, and makes gluttons out of orchard and town.
The stars can stand for bees who gather this
Luminous stuff that cloys the very trellises.
And look, all saccharine as they pour from the skies,
The rays of the moon are in fact honey-rays,
Hidden gold. I dream of some sugary happening,
But I fear the bee Arcturus and his fiery sting,
Who having put these slippery beams in my hands
Took his lunar honey from the rose of the winds.

(Tr. by William Meredith)

IN DISPRAISE OF THE MOON

by Mary Coleridge

(1861–1907)

I would not be the Moon, the sickly thing,
To summon owls and bats upon the wing;
For when the noble Sun is gone away,
She turns his night into a pallid day.

She hath no air, no radiance of her own,
That world unmusical of earth and stone.
She wakes her dim, uncolored, voiceless hosts,
Ghost of the Sun, herself the sun of ghosts.

The mortal eyes that gaze too long on her
Of Reason's piercing ray defrauded are.
Light in itself doth feed the living brain;
That light, reflected, but makes darkness plain.

MADMAN'S SONG

by Elinor Wylie

(1885–1928)

Better to see your cheek grown hollow,
Better to see your temple worn,
Than to forget to follow, follow,
After the sound of a silver horn.

Better to bind your brow with willow
And follow, follow until you die,
Than to sleep with your head on a golden pillow,
Nor lift it up when the hunt goes by.

Better to see your cheek grown sallow,
And your hair grown gray, so soon, so soon,
Than to forget to hallo, hallo,
After the milk-white hounds of the moon.

TOM O' BEDLAM'S SONG

(*Anonymous ballad*)

From the hagg and hungrie goblin
That into raggs would rend ye,
And the spirit that stands by the naked man
In the Book of Moones defend yee!
That of your five sounde sences
You never be forsaken,
Nor wander from your selves with Tom
Abroad to begg your bacon.
 While I doe sing "Any foode, any feeding,
 Feeding, drinke, or clothing,"
 Come dame or maid, be not afraid,
 Poor Tom will injure nothing.

Of thirty bare yeares have I
Twice twenty bin enragéd,
And of forty bin three tymes fifteene
In durance soundlie cagéd.
On the lordlie loftes of Bedlam,
With stubble softe and dainty,
Braue braceletts strong, sweep whips ding-dong,
With wholsome hunger plenty.
 And nowe I sing, etc.

With a thought I tooke for Maudlin,
And a cruse of cockle pottage,
With a thing thus tall, skie blesse you all,
I befell into this dotage.
I slept not since the Conquest,
Till then I never waked,
Till the rogysh boy of love where I lay
Mee found and strip't mee naked.
 And nowe I sing, etc.

When I short have shorne my sowre face
And swigg'd my horny barrel,
In an oaken inne I pound my skin
As a suite of gilt apparell.
The moon's my constant Mistrisse,
And the lowlie owle my morrowe,
The flaming Drake and the Nightcrowe make
Mee musicke to my sorrowe.
    While I doe sing, etc.

The palsie plagues my pulses
When I prigg your pigs or pullen,
Your culvers take, or matchles make
Your Chanticleare, or sullen.
When I want provant, with Humfrie
I sup, and when benighted,
I repose in Powles with waking soules
Yet nevere am affrighted.
    But I doe sing, etc.

I knowe more then Apollo,
For oft, when hee ly's sleeping,
I see the starres att bloudie warres
In the wounded welkin weeping;
The moone embrace her shepheard,
And the quene of Love her warryor,
While the first doth borne the star of morne,
And the next the heavenly Farrier.
    While I doe sing, etc.

The Gipsie snap and Pedro
Are none of Tom's comradoes.
The punk I skorne and the cut-purse sworn
And the roaring boyes bravadoe.
The meeke, the white, the gentle,
Me handle touch and spare not
But those that cross Tom Rynosseros
Doe what the panther dare not.
    Although I sing, etc.

) 117 (

With an host of furious fancies,
Whereof I am commander,
With a burning speare, and a horse of aire,
To the wildernesse I wander.
By a knight of ghostes and shadowes
I summon'd am to tourney
Ten leagues beyond the wide world's end.
Mee thinke it is noe journey.
    Yet I will sing "Any foode, any feeding,
    Feeding, drinke or clothing,"
    Come dame or maid, be not afraid,
    Poor Tom will injure nothing.

GIVING THE MOON A NEW CHANCE

by Terry Stokes

(1943–   )

I want to give my babies to the moon.
I donate my babies to the moon.
I surrender my babies to the moon.
I want them on the dark side.
Out of the sun. They get too much sun.
Always too much. I want their tears
to have no shadows. I don't want anybody
to bother my babies. I don't want them
to learn anything, & no thunder crash
in their eyes.

WHO DOTH NOT SEE
THE MEASURE OF THE MOON?

by Sir John Davies

(1569–1626)

Who doth not see the measure of the moon?
   Which thirteen times she danceth every year,
And ends her pavan thirteen times as soon
     As doth her brother, of whose golden hair
     She borroweth part, and proudly doth it wear.
       Then doth she coyly turn her face aside,
       That half her cheek is scarce sometimes descried.

Next her, the pure, subtle, and cleansing fire
     Is swiftly carried in a circle even,
Though Vulcan be pronounced by many a liar
     The only halting god that dwells in heaven;
     But that foul name may be more fitly given
       To your false fire, that far from heaven is fall,
       And doth consumer, waste, spoil, disorder all. . . .

"THE SUN SET, AND UP ROSE THE YELLOW MOON"

(from "Don Juan," stanzas 113–114)

by George Gordon, Lord Byron

(1788–1824)

The sun set, and up rose the yellow moon:
    The devil's in the moon for mischief; they
Who call'd her CHASTE, methinks, began too soon
    Their nomenclature; there is not a day,
The longest, not the twenty-first of June,
    Sees half the business in a wicked way
On which three single hours of moonshine smile—
And then she looks so modest all the while.

There is a dangerous silence in that hour,
    A stillness, which leaves room for the full soul
To open all itself, without the power
    Of calling wholly back its self-control;
The silver light which, hallowing tree and tower,
    Sheds beauty and deep softness o'er the whole,
Breathes also to the heart, and o'er it throws
A loving languor, which is not repose.

THE LUNAR TIDES

by Marya Zaturenska

(*1902–*   )

Danger stalks on such nights, the moon is dangerous:
Why will you walk beneath the compelling luster
That draws the blood from your unwilling body?
The vampire moon with yellow streams of light
Drains the dim waters, sucks the moist air dry,
Casts cloudy spectres on the window pane—
The dead arise and walk again.

Oh, love, how are we drawn
Into this moon, this face as cold,
Remorseless as ambition, chilled with fever,
Burning with war that on these lunar tides
Draws all life to its danger; beautiful
It mocks the living glory of the sun;
Such golden, flowing motion, dipping in perilous play
Forgets the warm assurances of day.

Resistance dies, is plucked so gently from
Our paralyzed wills, we hardly know it gone.
We are surrendered to the moon:
The light compels us, pole-stars to its orbit,
We shine in darkness fixed, invisible.
Too late for the last withdrawal, we are lost
In the intricacies of yellow frost.

Fantasies in the brain, restlessness in the heart,
Desire for the unattainable, the pure romantic longing—
Ruined towers in the air, a yearning toward the sea,
For its deep death, so cool, and languorous:
These are the favorite symptoms written down;
The pressure of the moon on the rare spirit,
The wild attraction and the deep repulsion,
The irresistible compulsion.

Dogs bark invisible terror, the trees loom sharply,
These ague glamours shake down mortal ill;
The wind beloved by lunatics and lovers
Descends and sways the grass, compels the lost
Disheveled light as sharp as silver daggers,
Such light as never from Olympus poured
But dark Judean light, sorrowful, pain-extolling
And Christian light, the Gothic thunder rolling.

"LADY, BY YONDER BLESSED MOON I SWEAR"

(From "Romeo and Juliet," II, 2)

by William Shakespeare

(1564–1616)

ROMEO:
Lady, by yonder blessed moon I swear,
That tips with silver all these fruit-tree tops—

JULIET:
Oh, swear not by the moon, th' inconstant moon,
That monthly changes in her circled orb,
Lest that thy love prove likewise variable.

THE SADNESS OF THE MOON

by Charles Baudelaire

(1821–1848)

The Moon more indolently dreams tonight
Than a fair woman on her couch at rest,
Caressing, with a hand distraught and light,
Before she sleeps, the contour of her breast.

Upon her silken avalanche of down,
Dying she breathes a long and swooning sigh;
And watches the white visions past her flown,
Which rise like blossoms to the azure sky.

And when, at times, wrapped in her languor deep,
Earthward she lets a furtive tear-drop flow,
Some pious poet, enemy of sleep,

Takes in his hollow hand the tear of snow
Whence gleams of iris and of opal start,
And hides it from the Sun, deep in his heart.

(Tr. by F. P. Trurm)

SUN OF THE SLEEPLESS!

by George Gordon, Lord Byron

(1788–1824)

Sun of the sleepless! melancholy star!
Whose tearful beam glows tremulously far,
That show'st the darkness thou canst not dispel,
How like art thou to Joy remembered well!
So gleams the past, the light of other days,
Which shines, but warms not with its powerless rays:
A night-beam, Sorrow watcheth to behold,
Distinct, but distant—clear—but, oh how cold!

TO THE MOON

by George Darley

(1795–1846)

Ay! thou look'st cold on me, pomp-loving Moon,
  Thy courtier stars following in bright array,
Like some proud queen, when Meekness begs a boon,
  With upraised brow wondering what he should say,—
  Then passing in her slow and silent scorn away!
Blank-visaged, wan, high-pacing Dame! I come,
  No suitor to thy pity; nor to crave
One beam to gild the darkness of my doom,
  Not even a tear to weep me in the grave;
Think'st thou I'd wear thy tinsel on my pall,
  Or deck my shroud with sorry gems like thine?
No, let me die, unseen, unwept of all,
  Let not a dog over my ashes whine,—
  And sweep thou on thy worldly way, O Moon! nor glance at mine!

CLAIR DE LUNE

by Paul Verlaine

(1841–1896)

Your soul is a sealed garden, and there go
With masque and bergamasque fair companies
Playing on lutes and dancing and as though
Sad under their fantastic fripperies.

Though they in minor keys go carolling
Of love the conqueror and of life the boon
They seem to doubt the happiness they sing
And the song melts into the light of the moon,

The sad light of the moon, so lovely fair
That all the birds dream in the leafy shade
And the slim fountains sob into the air
Among the marble statues in the glade.

(Tr. by Arthur Symons)

LOOK DOWN FAIR MOON

by Walt Whitman

(1819–1892)

Look down fair moon and bathe this scene,
Pour softly down night's nimbus floods on faces ghastly,
   swollen, purple,
On the dead on their backs with arms toss'd wide,
Pour down your unstinted nimbus sacred moon.

MOONLIGHT

by Henry Wadsworth Longfellow

(*1807–1882*)

As a pale phantom with a lamp
    Ascends some ruin's haunted stair,
So glides the moon along the damp
    Mysterious chambers of the air.

Now hidden in cloud, and now revealed,
    As if this phantom, full of pain,
Were by the crumbling walls concealed,
    And at the windows seen again.

Until at last, serene and proud
    In all the splendor of her light,
She walks the terraces of cloud,
    Supreme as Empress of the Night.

I look, but recognize no more
    Objects familiar to my view;
The very pathway to my door
    Is an enchanted avenue.

All things are changed. One mass of shade,
    The elm-trees drop their curtains down;
By palace, park, and colonnade
    I walk as in a foreign town.

The very ground beneath my feet
    Is clothed with a diviner air;
While marble paves the silent street
    And glimmers in the empty square.

Illusion! Underneath there lies
    The common life of every day;
Only the spirit glorifies
    With its own tints the somber gray.

In vain we look, in vain uplift
    Our eyes to heaven, if we are blind;
We see but what we have the gift
    Of seeing; what we bring we find.

MOON SONG, WOMAN SONG

by Anne Sexton

(1928–   )

I am alive at night.
I am dead in the morning,
an old vessel who used up her oil,
bleak and pale boned.
No miracle. No dazzle.
I'm out of repair
but you are tall in your battle dress
and I must arrange for your journey.
I was always a virgin,
old and pitted.
Before the world was, I was.

I have been oranging and fat,
carrot colored, gaped at,
allowing my cracked o's to drop on the sea
near Venice and Mombasa.
Over Maine I have rested.
I have fallen like a jet into the Pacific.
I have committed perjury over Japan.
I have dangled my pendulum,
my fat bag, my gold, gold,
blinkedy light
over you all.

So if you must inquire, do so.
After all I am not artificial.
I looked long upon you,
love-bellied and empty,
flipping my endless display
for you, you my cold, cold
coverall man.

You need only request
and I will grant it.
It is virtually guaranteed
that you will walk into me like a barracks.
So come cruising, come cruising,
you of the blast off,
you of the bastion,
you of the scheme.
I will shut my fat eye down,
headquarters of an area,
house of a dream.

"BUT, SOFT! WHAT LIGHT THROUGH YONDER WINDOW BREAKS?"

(from "Romeo and Juliet," II, 2)

by *William Shakespeare*

(*1564–1616*)

ROMEO:

But, soft! What light through yonder window breaks?
It is the east, and Juliet is the sun!
Arise, fair sun, and kill the envious moon,
Who is already sick and pale with grief
That thou her maid art far more fair than she.
Be not her maid, since she is envious.
Her vestal livery is but sick and green,
And none but fools do wear it. Cast it off.
It is my lady, oh, it is my love!

THE SETTING OF THE MOON

by Giacomo Leopardi

(1798–1837)

As in the lonely night,
Above the waters and the silvered plains,
Where fluttering breezes move,
And distant shadows feign
A thousand images,
Illusory and fair,
Among the quiet waves,
Hedgerows, and trees, and hills, and villages—
Having reached the sky's confine,
Past Apennine, or Alp, or in the Tyrrhene
Sea's unsounded bosom,
The moon descends, and all the world grows dim,
The shadows disappear,
And one same darkness blots out vale and mountain.
While night remains, bereaved,
And singing, with a mournful melody,
The wagoner hails the last gleam of that light
Which now is vanishing
And on his journey still had been his guide;

Thus disappears, even so
From human life must go,
The season of youth. Away
Depart the shadowy forms
And beautiful illusions; less now seem
Those far-off hopes on which
Our suffering mortal nature learned to lean.
Desolate, full of darkness,
Our life remains. And gazing round on it,
Bewildered, vainly would the traveller trace
On the long round which lies before him yet
Reason or bourn; he finds
That he has now become

A stranger here where dwells the human race.
Too sweet, too full of joy,
Had seemed our mortal state
To those above, if our first youthful time,
Whose every good is bred from thousand pains,
Had lasted out the whole course of our life.
Too mild were that decree
Which sentences to death each living thing,
Did not the path to it,
Though half completed yet,
First show itself more harsh than terrible death.
The Eternal Ones devised
The last of all our ills,
Worthy invention of immortal minds,—
Old age, where still desire
Survives, with hope extinct,
When pleasure's founts run dry, and every pain
Grows more and more, while good comes not again.

You, banks and little hills,
Though hidden be the light which from the west
Had silvered all the mantle of the night,
Orphaned you shall not long
Remain, for very soon you may discern
Once more the eastern skies
Grow pale with morning, till the dawn arise,
Whom the sun follows after, and comes forth,
Blazing and bright again,
And with its ardent beams,
His shining streams of light,
Floods all your summits and the ethereal plain.
But mortal life, when the fair time of youth
Has vanished, never then grows bright again
With any radiance more, or second dawn.
Widowed until the end; and in the night,
Where through the dark we come,
The gods have set a sign for us, the tomb.

(*Tr. by John Heath-Stubbs*)

LUNAR PARAPHRASE

by *Wallace Stevens*

(*1878–1955*)

The moon is the mother of pathos and pity.

When, at the wearier end of November,
Her old light moves along the branches,
Feebly, slowly, depending upon them;
When the body of Jesus hangs in a pallor,
Humanly near, and the figure of Mary,
Touched on by hoar-frost, shrinks in a shelter
Made by the leaves, that have rotted and fallen;
When over the houses, a golden illusion
Brings back an earlier season of quiet
And quieting dreams in the sleepers in darkness—

The moon is the mother of pathos and pity.

THE MOON AND THE YEW TREE

by Sylvia Plath

(*1932–1962*)

This is the light of the mind, cold and planetary.
The trees of the mind are black. The light is blue.
The grasses unload their griefs on my feet as if I were God,
Prickling my ankles and murmuring of their humility.
Fumey, spiritous mists inhabit this place
Separated from my house by a row of headstones.
I simply cannot see where there is to get to.

The moon is no door. It is a face in its own right,
White as a knuckle and terribly upset.
It drags the sea after it like a dark crime; it is quiet
With the O-gape of complete despair. I live here.
Twice on Sunday, the bells startle the sky—
Eight great tongues affirming the Resurrection.
At the end, they soberly bong out their names.

The yew tree points up. It has a Gothic shape.
The eyes lift after it and find the moon.
The moon is my mother. She is not sweet like Mary.
Her blue garments unloose small bats and owls.
How I would like to believe in tenderness—
The face of the effigy, gentled by candles,
Bending, on me in particular, its mild eyes.

I have fallen a long way. Clouds are flowering
Blue and mystical over the face of the stars.
Inside the church, the saints will be all blue,
Floating on their delicate feet over the cold pews,
Their hands and faces stiff with holiness.
The moon sees nothing of this. She is bald and wild.
And the message of the yew tree is blackness—blackness
  and silence.

VI

AFTER APOLLO

VOYAGE TO THE MOON

by Archibald MacLeish

(1892–   )

Presence among us,
wanderer in our skies,
dazzle of silver in our leaves and on our
waters silver,
O silver evasion in our farthest thought—
"the visiting moon" . . . "the glimpses of the moon" . . .
and we have touched you!

From the first of time,
before the first of time, before the
first men tasted time, we thought of you.
You were a wonder to us, unattainable,
a longing past the reach of longing,
a light beyond our light, our lives—perhaps
a meaning to us.

Now our hands have touched you in your depth
of night.

Three days and three nights we journeyed,
steered by farthest stars, climbed outward,
crossed the invisible tide-rip where the floating dust
falls one way or the other in the void between,
followed that other dawn, encountered
cold, faced death—unfathomable emptiness . . .
Then, the fourth day evening, we descended,
made fast, set foot at dawn upon your beaches,
sifted between our fingers your cold sand.

We stand here in the dusk, the cold, the silence . . .

and here, as at the first of time, we lift our heads.
Over us, more beautiful than the moon, a

moon, a wonder to us, unattainable,
a longing past the reach of longing,
a light beyond our light, our lives—perhaps
a meaning to us . . .

O, a meaning!

Over us on these silent beaches the bright
earth,
      presence among us.

VOYAGE TO THE MOON

by William Dickey

(*1928–*   )

Of that world, having returned from it, I may say
There is no romance there, no air of being present
To carry the sound of compliment. The inhabitants
Cannot smell one another, even when the sun
At long midday heats them beyond our temperature.

It is therefore a nation of pure philosophy
Without sin or absolution. The swift works
Of their brains show through their crystal faces
With absolute consonance. The pattern of their thoughts
Is like that of pleased clocks agreeing on an hour.

They are advanced in mathematics. The closest thing
To affection I could observe among them was
The appreciation of a theorem shared by two
Investigators. The emotion was expressed
By a formal, rapid exchanging of prime numbers.

The air of earth would surely be fatal to them,
Our sounds shatter, our perfumes corrode them. But
What would bring them, I think, most entirely to a stop
Would be to watch our explosions of hate and love
Which may serve as armament for the next expedition.

NINE BEAN-ROWS ON THE MOON

by Al Purdy

(1918–   )

No woman has ever lost her man
to another woman here
or had him just go
because he didn't want to stay any longer
No woman has spent the night rocking in pain
knowing that even in her grave and later
she will not see him again
The grief of a child's death has not touched
this place
or the dumb grandeur of mourning for the lost
                And the inconsolable
walkers in the storm
cursing at the locked gates of fact
refuse to be satisfied with fiction
board a leaky ship for the past
not to be seen again among us
except as our knowledge that pain and death
have their own glory that lifts them
sometimes over our limitations
of being dust to dust
but more than human

After the landing
on that torn landscape of the mind
and the first steps are taken
let a handful of moon-dust run thru your hand
and escape back to itself
for those others
the ghosts of grief and loss
walking beyond the Sea of Serenity

STRANGE KIND (II)

by J. D. Reed

(1940–   )

They lied about
photos
of her other side

it's hollow
just burnt struts
and shreds of velvet
waving slowly
in the anti-wind of space
a sham
theatre of a globe

She sits there
on her throne
clacking her beak
chewing lovers

skin taut
on her dome
reflects on the gold
face-plate
of the floating
astronaut   this Jason
of the vacuum

TO THE MOON AND BACK

by William Plomer

(1903–   )

countdown	takeoff
moonprints	rockbox
splashdown	claptrap

A FAREWELL, A WELCOME

The moon age

by Lisel Mueller

(*1924–*   )

Goodbye pale cold inconstant
tease   you never existed
therefore we had to invent you

> Goodbye crooked little man
> huntress who sleeps alone
> dear pastor, shepherd of stars
> who tucked us in   goodbye
> sun's nubile runaway sister

Good riddance phony prop
con man moon
who tap-danced with June
to the tender surrender
of love from above

Goodbye decanter of magic liquids
fortune teller *par excellence*
seducer   incubus   medicine man
exile's sanity   love's sealed lips
womb that nourished the monstrous child
and the sweet rich grain   goodbye
> we trade you in as we traded
> the evil eye for the virus
> the rosy seat of affections
> for the indispensable pump

we say farewell as we said farewell
to angels in nightgowns   to Grandfather God

Goodbye forever Edam and Gorgonzola
cantaloupe in the sky
night-watchman, one-eyed loner
　　　　　nevertheless, wolves
　　　　　are programmed to howl　　goodbye
　　　　　forbidden lover goodbye
　　　　　sleepwalkers will wander
　　　　　with outstretched arms for no reason
　　　　　while you continue routinely
　　　　　to husband the sea, prevail
　　　　　in the fix of infant strabismus

Goodbye ripe ovum　　women will spill their blood
in spite of you now　　lunatics wave goodbye
accepting despair by another name

Welcome new world to the brave old words
peace　　hope　　justice
truth everlasting　　welcome
ash-colored playground of children
happy in airy bags
never to touch is never to miss it

Scarface hello we've got you covered
welcome untouchable　　vagrant
with an alias in every country
salvos and roses　　you are home
　　and we still cast shadows

APOLLO 8

by John Berryman

(1914–1972)

Bizarre Apollo, half what Henry dreamed,
half real, wandered back on stage from the other wing
with its incredible circuitry.
All went well. The moon? What the moon seemed
to Henry in his basement: shadows gathering
around an archaic sea

with craters grand on the television screen,
as dead as Delphi treeless, tourist gone
& the god decidedly gone.
Selene slid by the Far-Shooter, mean
of plagues & arrows, whom the doom clampt on,
both embarrassed in the Christian dawn.

(That roar you hear as the rocket lifts is money, hurt.)

Which dawn has ended, and it is full day.
And the mountain of Mao flesh, did it once respond
'Let all moons bloom'? O no,
these events are for kids & selenographers, say,
a deep breath, creating no permanent bond
between the passive watchers & moonglow.

IN A MOONLIT HERMIT'S CABIN
by *Allen Ginsberg*
(*1926–*)

Watching the White Image, electric moon, white mist drifting
over woods
St. John's Wort & Hawkeye wet with chance Yarrow on the green
hillside
"D'ya want your Airline Transport Pilot to smoke grass? Want
yr moon-men to smoke loco weed?"
What Comedy's this Epic! The lamb lands on the Alcohol Sea—
Deep voices
"A Good batch of Data"—The hours of Man's first landing on the
moon—
One and a Half Million starv'd in Biafra—Football players
broadcast cornflakes—
TV mentioned America as much as Man—Brillo offers you free
Moon-Map—2 labels—
And CBS repeats Man-Epic—Now here again is Walter Cronkite,
"How easy these words . . . a shiver down the old spine . . .
Russia soundly beaten! China one Fifth of Mankind, no word
broadcast . . ."
The Queen watched the moon-landing at Windsor Castle—
Pulling a fast one on Hypnosis at Disneyland, the Kerchief-headed
Crowd
Waving to the TV Camera—Ersatz Moon—
"No place gives you history today except the Moon"—
Running behind time entering Space Suits—
And a Moon-in at Central Sheep Meadow—
Western Electric's solemn moment!

And rain in the woods drums on the old cabin!
I want! I want! a ladder from the depths of the forest night to the
silvery moon-wink—
A flag on the reporter's space-suit shoulder—
Peter Groaning & Cursing in bed, relieved of the lunatic burden at
last—

'Tis Tranquillity base where the Tragedy will settle the Eve.
Alert for solar flares, clock ticks, static from Antennae—swift as
    death.
I didn't think we'd see this Night.
Plant the flag and you're doomed! Life a dream—slumber in eyes
    of woods,
Antennae scraping the ceiling. Static & Rain!
Saw the earth in Dream age 37, half cloud-wrapped, from a
    balcony in outer-space—
Méliès—giddiness—picture tube gaga—
"Men land on Sun!" decennial sentences—
Announcers going goofy muttering "142—"
Alone in space: Dump Pressure in the LEM!
Hare Krishna! Lift m'Dorje on the kitchen table!
No Science Fiction expected this Globe-Eye Consciousness
Simultaneous with opening a hatch on Heaven.
A moth in the Déjà Vu!
This is the instant—open the hatch—every second is dust in the
    hourglass—Hatch open!
The Virus will grow green slime reptiles in sixty centuries,
& gobble up their fathers as we ate up God—
Imagine dying Tonight! Closing the eyes on the man in the
    Moon!
Sighing away forever . . . everyone got sleepy . . . On the
    moon porch—

A 38 year old human American standing on the surface of the
    moon—
Footprint on the Charcoal dust—stepped out
and it's the old familiar Moon, as undersea or mountain-top, a
    place—
"Very pretty on the Moon!" oh, 'twere Solid Gold—
Voices calling "Houston to Moon"—Two "Americans" on the
    moon!
Beautiful view, bouncing the surface—"one quarter of the world
    denied these pix by their rulers"!
Setting up the flag!

July Moon Day '69

[MOONSHOT]

by Robert Kelly

(1935–   )

It does not matter
that an immense bureaucracy
neglectful of the needs of men themselves
of earth itself
put them there

it matters that human
breath will shape
utterance on the unconscious moon
wake it
& us
from the bitter long dream of silence
by breath
of a man's body
by the weight of his weight
breath
breathed into the moon

the sound of it,
making an atmos be
will some day hear us
as we have not yet heard
Adam in Eden
& yet we grow
& our breath
goes before us
shaping the matter of all energies
to our one energy

AESTHETICS OF THE MOON

by *Jack Anderson*

(*1935–*   )

It is so pure, so complete
-ly nothing
      it is the absolute
         work of art:
            unparaphraseable and self-contained

it just hangs up there
    more permanent
       than anything on earth
              (where *The Last Supper*
                  has faded already)
it stays as it is: perfect, perfectly wrought
    the solid hermetic emptiness
       which is ultimate form

To set foot on it
    even once
       is to corrupt it utterly:

       a jolly hiker
       with binoculars and cheese sandwiches
       bursting with a yodel
       through the *Mona Lisa's* smile
       the canvas ripped
       beyond repair
       Hi there!
       now that I am here
       it no longer exists: instead
       I exist on it
       To know that I am here
       on it, destroying it
       step by step
       is the new kind of art work in your mind

and once I come back to you
that, too,
will no longer be

"But can you not at least record what you saw and felt
the moment you touched that still untarnished place?"

Sure thing:
you know me
how we grew up together
went to the same high school
dated the same girls, monkeyed with cars

you know how I see things
(or maybe you don't
I can't quite recollect)

Anyway, how I see it is:
rocks   lots of rocks
dust   lots of dust
rocks and dust   lots everywhere
quite a sight   but nothing like home
you can take my word for that

"Such persistent blandness of thought!
such unwholesome wholesomeness!
as though engaged in making your life worthy
of a small town on television!"

So who else should be sent   who could do it
some alcoholic dope-freak   guitar-picking hustler
burglar   mugger?
oh no   what we do requires
not flights of imagination
but holding on

I've been someplace and seen it
the only way I know how
it's up to you to do something about it

) 154 (

It's a place now like Siberia or Yellowstone
no longer form it's real estate it's
a site for
whatever comes next
a raw material

THE LUNAR PROBE

by Maxine Kumin

(1925–   )

Long before morning they waked me to say
the moon was undone; had blown out, sky high,
swelled fat as a fat pig's bladder, fit
to burst, and then the underside had split.

I had been dreaming this dream seven nights
before it bore fruit (there is nothing so sweet
to a prophet as forethought come true). They had meant
merely to prick when . . . good-bye, good intent!

Dozing, I saw the sea stopper its flux,
dogs freeze in mid-howl, women wind up their clocks,
lunatics everywhere sane as their keepers.

I have not dreamed since in this nation of sleepers.

LUNE CONCRÈTE

by Raymond Federman

(1928–   )

```
I have not yet b          egun to relate y
ou dumb moon ston          es asleep in your
future dust and wh          at could be said o
f your stubborn sle          ep silent little wo
rlds that one should          listen dream contemp
late your dusty destr          uction and yet I awai
t that which will be s   aid of the cold passio
nate moment that precedes all rupture the noth
ing yet ex   pressed of the softn   ess of you
r name and   carelessness of yo   ur form an
d the mean   inglessness of y   our dark t
exture you      - MOONSTONES -      or simplex
stones pie       ces of falle       n moon sto
len and wh        ich remain        to be expl
ained touc         hed deco         mposed sil
ently in t          he lig          ht since o
ne must in           rent           you create
you silenc            e             you before
one can th                          ink you sp
eak you to                          awake your
dust out o                          f its dumb
moon exist                          ence now t
hat you ha        00000000         ve reached
the terres        0      0         tial space
                  0      0
                  0      0
                  0      0
                  0      0
                  00000000


                  00000000
                  0      0
                  0      0
                  0      0
                  0      0
                  0      0
                  00000000


                N        N
                N N      N
                N   N    N
                N     N  N
                N      N N
                N        N
```

) 157 (

VACUUM

by Josephine Miles

(*1911–*   )

We are already on the moon,
We make such minerals in the vacuum
Furnace of the electric beam.
Their molecules together run
One every mile, in density
And pressure of the lunar cone.

In the new lab down on the waterfront
The tides of moon draw, fibres of the heart
Compress, constrict, till from this metal shape
Flows out a foil as thin and consequent
As moon on water and as moon on wing,
As moon on man the gold foil of his brain.

THE FLIGHT OF APOLLO

by Stanley Kunitz

(*1905–*   )

I

Earth was my home, but even there I was a stranger. This mineral crust. I walk like a swimmer. What titanic bombardments in those old astral wars! I know what I know: I shall never escape from strangeness or complete my journey. Think of me as nostalgic, afraid, exalted. I am your man on the moon, a speck of megalomania, restless for the leap towards island universes pulsing beyond where the constellations set. Infinite space overwhelms the human heart, but in the middle of nowhere life inexorably calls to life. Forward my mail to Mars. What news from the Great Spiral Nebula in Andromeda and the Magellanic Clouds?

II

I was a stranger on earth.
Stepping on the moon, I begin
the gay pilgrimage to new
Jerusalems
in foreign galaxies.
Heat. Cold. Craters of silence.
The Sea of Tranquillity
rolling on the shores of entropy.
And, beyond,
the intelligence of the stars.

SPACE

by X. J. Kennedy

(*1929–*   )

(FOR MARTIN GREEN)

I

Who could have thought, but for eight days in space,
The heart might learn to thrive on weightlessness,
As though with no flesh holding it in place,
Yearning by choice, not made to by distress,
Turning in free fall on reprieve from earth
We tug-of-war with daily for the sakes
Of those we long for, those we help bring forth.
How will it be when all the strength it takes
To rip moons loose from planet boughs, or send
Engines of slag careening from their track
Into the unending dark, end over slow end,
Is in the twist that opens a door a crack?
Who will need long to savor his desire
When wishes no more blunt them against bulk,
But pierce straight through; when acts, once dreamt, transpire?
Man may imagine man's own mother's milk.

II

Heads bowed in fetal crouch, the Gemini
Float in their pear-shaped comfort. Data grows
By little clicks, as pine cones, drying free
And dropping, pile up. Enter, through a hose,
Essence of roast beef. Signs that flash ABORT
Bespeak a tube's break. If all hold, instead,
The moon's thin skin shall cringe under their boots—
Just as we always thought, the thing's stone dead.

III

Hope to be disembodied reconciles
Our drifted hearts to that exacting beat.
We clerks-without-church look on while slide-rules
Render our lusts and madnesses concrete.
It may well be that when I rev my car
And let it overtake and pass my thinking,
It's space I crave; when my electric bar
Sets up a moonshot, lemon-oiled and clinking,
And gulp by gulp, I shrug the world's dull weight,
Out after what I had long thought I'd hate.

MOON LANDING

by W. H. Auden

(1907–1973)

It's natural the Boys should whoop it up for
so huge a phallic triumph, an adventure
    it would not have occurred to women
    to think worth while, made possible only

because we like huddling in gangs and knowing
the exact time: yes, our sex may in fairness
    hurrah the deed, although the motives
    that primed it were somewhat less than *menschlich*.

A grand gesture. But what does it period?
What does it osse? We were always adroiter
    with objects than lives, and more facile
    at courage than kindness: from the moment

the first flint was flaked this landing was merely
a matter of time. But our selves, like Adam's,
    still don't fit us exactly, modern
    only in this—our lack of decorum.

Homer's heroes were certainly no braver
than our Trio, but more fortunate: Hector
    was excused the insult of having
    his valor covered by television.

Worth *going* to see? I can well believe it.
Worth *seeing?* Mneh! I once rode through a desert
    and was not charmed: give me a watered
    lively garden, remote from blatherers

about the New, the von Brauns and their ilk, where
on August mornings I can count the morning
    glories, where to die has a meaning,
    and no engine can shift my perspective.

Unsmudged, thank God, my Moon still queens the Heavens
as She ebbs and fulls, a Presence to glop at,
        Her Old Man, made of grit not protein,
        still visits my Austrian several

with His old detachment, and the old warnings
still have power to scare me: Hybris comes to
        an ugly finish, Irreverence
        is a greater oaf than Superstition.

Our apparatniks will continue making
the usual squalid mess called History:
        all we can pray for is that artists,
        chefs and saints still appear to blithe it.

MOON MAN

by Jean Valentine

(*1934–*   )

'*Here too we dare to hope.*'
—Romano Guardini

FOR A. R.

Swimming down to us
light years
not always a straight line
that was his joke, his night
fears, his pilgrim's climb.

About half way
throwing his silver
suit away he
sees the green earth
click for the first time:

the lightest girl
the heaviest ocean
coming to themselves
and to his hand.

He sets a comradely couple walking
down his white road,
hospitable; hears a shiny
boy and girl, bird and bird
having a time

in his green water.
Clean against it all
one last hour
all alone the moon man's
open everywhere:

This mass is his salt
his girl
        his sky
his work
        his floor.

EDITH SITWELL
ASSUMES THE ROLE OF LUNA
or
IF YOU KNOW WHAT I MEAN
SAID THE MOON

by Robert Francis

(*1901–*   )

Who (said the Moon)
Do you think I am and precisely who
Pipsqueak, are you

With your uncivil liberties
To do as you damn please?
Boo!

I am the serene
Moon (said the Moon).
Don't touch me again.

To your poking telescopes,
Your peeking eyes
I have long been wise.

Science? another word
For monkeyshine.
You heard me.

Get down, little man, go home,
Back where you come from,
Bah!

Or my gold will be turning green
On me (said the Moon)
If you know what I mean.

VIEWS OF OUR SPHERE

by *Ernest Sandeen*

(*1908–*   )

We deserved that earth-shot from the
moon's asbestos-gray horizon: a
family portrait on the old homestead, yet
not a single one of us could be
seen and the only history being made was
storm-swirls over rocks and oceans.

So our prophets from as long ago as the
close of paradise had at last a
picture to illustrate their remarks.

As the atoms in our invisible heads
go on blasting out toward darker and
darker lights what can we hope for but
smaller and smaller snapshots of this place
already small and lonesome enough.

The countdown, however, is pulsing in all our
engineered spaces of mind, and each flight
now must explode into the next till
we and our shape in the sun and our weather
vanish altogether (all together).

AN OREGON MESSAGE

by William Stafford

(1914–   )

When we moved here, pulled
the trees in around us, curled
our backs to the wind, no one
had ever hit the moon—no one.
Now our trees are safer than the stars,
and only other people's neglect
is our precious and abiding shell,
pierced by meteors, radar, and the telephone.

From our snug place we shout
religiously for attention, in order to hide;
only silence or evasion will bring
dangerous notice, the hovering hawk
of the state, or the sudden quiet stare
and fatal estimate of an alerted neighbor.

This message we smuggle out in
its plain cover, to be opened
quietly: Friends, everywhere—
we are alive! Those moon rockets
have missed millions of secret
places! Best wishes.

Burn this.

TO THE MOON, 1969

by Babette Deutsch

(1895–   )

You are not looked for through the smog, you turn blindly
Behind that half palpable poison—you who no longer
Own a dark side, yet whose radiance falters, as if it were
    fading.
Now you have been reached, you are altered
                      beyond belief—
As a stranger spoken to, remaining remote, changes from being
    a stranger.
Astronomers know you a governor of tides, women as the mistress
Of menstrual rhythms, poets have called you Hecate, Astarte,
    Artemis—huntress whose arrows
Fuse into a melt of moonlight as they pour
                    upon earth, upon water.
We all know you a danger
    to the thief in the garden, the pilot
In the enemy plane, to lovers embraced in your promise
    of a shining security. Are you a monster?
A noble being? Or simply a planet that men have, almost casually,
    cheapened?
The heavens do not answer.
Once, it was said, the cry: "Pan is dead! Great Pan is dead!"
    shivered, howled, through the forests: the gentle
Christ had killed him.
There is no lament for you—who are silent
    as the dead always are.
You have left the mythologies, the old ones, our own.
But, for a few, what has happened is the death of a divine
    Person, is a betrayal, is a piece of
The cruelty that the Universe feeds
                while displaying its glories.

THE MOON GROUND

by James Dickey

(1923–   )

You look as though
You know me, though the world we came from is striking
     You in the forehead like Apollo. Buddy,
We have brought the gods. We know what it is to shine
     Far off, with earth. We alone
          Of all men, could take off
Our shoes and fly. One-sixth of our weight, we have
          gathered,
     Both of us, under another one
Of us overhead. He is reading the dials he is understanding
     Time, to save our lives. You and I are in earth
     light and deep moon
       shadow on magic ground
Of the dead new world, and we do not but we could
Leap over each other like children in the universal
     playground
     Of stones
         but we must not play
    At being here: we must look
     We must look for it: the stones are going to tell us
Not the why but the how of all things. Brother, your gold
    face flashes
On me. It is the earth. I hear your deep voice rumbling from the
  body
     Of its huge clothes. Why did we come here
     It does not say, but the ground looms, and the secret
       Of time is lying
      Within amazing reach. It is everywhere
   We walk, our glass heads shimmering with absolute
   heat
       And cold. We leap slowly
    Along it. We will take back the very stones

Of Time, and build it where we live. Or in the cloud
striped blue of home, will the secret crumble
In our hands with air? Will the moon-plague kill our children
In their beds? The Human Planet trembles in its black
Sky with what we do   I can see it hanging in the god-gold only
Brother of your face. We are this world: we are
The only men. What hope is there at home
In the azure breath, or here with the stone
Dead secret? My massive clothes bubble around me
Crackling with static and Gray's
Elegy helplessly coming
From my heart, and I say I think something
From high school I remember Now
Fades the glimmering landscape on the sight, and all the air
A solemn stillness holds. Earth glimmers
And in its air-color a solemn stillness holds
it. O brother! Earth-faced god! APOLLO! My eyes blind
With unreachable tears   my breath goes all over
Me and cannot escape. We are here to do one
Thing only, and that is rock by rock to carry the moon to
take it
Back. Our clothes embrace we cannot touch we cannot
Kneel. We stare into the moon
dust, the earth-blazing ground. We laughed with the
beautiful craze
Of static. We bend, we pick up stones.

LANDING ON THE MOON
by May Swenson
(1927–   )

When in the mask of night there shone that cut,
we were riddled. A probe reached down
and stroked some nerve in us,
as if the glint from a wizard's eye, of silver,
slanted out of the mask of the unknown—
pit of riddles, the scratch-marked sky.

When, albino bowl on cloth of jet,
it spilled its virile rays,
our eyes enlarged, our blood reared with the waves.
We craved its secret, but unreachable
it held away from us, chilly and frail.
Distance kept it magnate. Enigma made it white.

When we learned to read it with our rod,
reflected light revealed
a lead mirror, a bruised shield
seamed with scars and shadow-soiled.
A half-faced sycophant, its glitter borrowed,
rode around our throne.

On the moon there shines earth light
as moonlight shines upon the earth . . .
If on its obsidian we set our weightless foot,
and sniff no wind, and lick no rain
and feel no gauze between us and the Fire,
will we trot its grassless skull, sick for the homelike shade?

Naked to the earth-beam we will be,
who have arrived to map an apparition,
who walk upon the forehead of a myth.
Can flesh rub with symbol? If our ball
be iron, and not light, our earliest wish
eclipses. Dare we land upon a dream?

A FAREWELL TO THE MOON

by Ed Ochester
(1939–   )

Are these the astronauts who carried
the illicit letters to the moon?
one forgets so soon but
I'd like to be dressed in aluminum foil
and brought to you by Tang, and brought closer
to God, whose face is seen in outer space
more clearly than on earth, and
brought to you by Tang.

But here a small child asks:
"How do the astronauts go to the bathroom?"
First their lunar rover breaks down and
they fix it with paper
and then pee through plastic tubes
into recycling machines in which
little is lost except for the salt and
then the water like racial memories is pumped
back into Tang

so that the footprints will be made
and last longer than the Third Reich's
supposed thousand years,
so that a golf ball will be whacked
a thousand yards so that the footprints
will be left wandering to rock outcroppings
so that, perhaps, alien eyes eons from now
will see purposeful strides leading
to the sullen backward black abysm of time
as
men now puzzle over
gigantic footprints frozen into rock
in California, leading to a waterhole
that millennia ago
had disappeared.

INDEX OF TITLES

INDEX OF
AUTHORS AND TRANSLATORS

INDEX OF FIRST LINES

) 179 (